John Cooper

Self-Sacrifice

The grandest manifestation of the divine, and the true principle of Christian life. Or,

the lost power of Christian zeal restored to the church

John Cooper

Self-Sacrifice

The grandest manifestation of the divine, and the true principle of Christian life. Or, the lost power of Christian zeal restored to the church

ISBN/EAN: 9783337222499

Printed in Europe, USA, Canada, Australia, Japan

Cover: Foto ©Lupo / pixelio.de

More available books at **www.hansebooks.com**

SELF-SACRIFICE:

THE GRANDEST MANIFESTATION OF THE DIVINE, AND THE TRUE PRINCIPLE OF CHRISTIAN LIFE;

OR,

THE LOST POWER OF CHRISTIAN ZEAL RESTORED TO THE CHURCH.

BY

REV. JOHN COOPER,

AUTHOR OF "THE SCIENCE OF SPIRITUAL LIFE," "THE PROVINCE OF LAW," "CHRIST'S MODE OF PRESENTING HIMSELF TO THE WORLD," ETC.

London:
HODDER AND STOUGHTON,
27, PATERNOSTER ROW.

MDCCCLXXX.

Hazell, Watson, and Viney, Printers, London and Aylesbury.

PREFACE.

SCEPTICISM is abroad; there is a rustling among the dry bones, a shaking of those things which are to be removed, that those things which cannot be shaken may remain. Anxiety is felt, fears expressed, and efforts put forth to meet what is regarded as the demand of the day. At all times there has been, is, and will be, commotion, agitation, and misgiving, and in such times it is especially incumbent on truth-seekers to distinguish between the real and enduring, the mutable and the evanescent of truth, between the body and soul of revelation. In every endeavour to meet what is felt to be the religious demand of the period, care must be taken to distinguish between the ritualistic and formal, and the spiritual of religious life. The one is necessarily mutable, the other essentially permanent.

Care also must be taken to distinguish between self-seeking and self-sacrificing in religious endeavours. The one, displaying itself in connection with the externals of religious life, will produce formalism, and secure disappointment and grief. The other, operating internally, will reveal itself in the life, and produce the loveliest phase of religious character, opening up the well-spring of pure bliss in the soul, and producing the most generous and beneficent deeds.

Religion is an embodied life. The religious creature must have devotion, rite, creed, ecclesiasticism, and forms of morality. As long as these forms are regarded as accidental and mutable, all is well. But if these are looked upon as essential and permanent, then mistake is fallen into, and evil in its direst forms incurred. The distinction between the embracing and manifesting the Divine in connection with and by means of the appointed instrumentalities, and the clinging to and resting in outer forms, must be ever carefully kept in view. If the forms of religious life are animated by the spirit of self-seeking, evil and only evil is and must be the result; but if these forms are animated by the spirit of self-sacrifice, all is and must be well.

The shaking of the formal in religious life is necessary to its progress in the spiritual. It is through tribulation that the kingdom is entered, that the Church and the believer ascend into the higher realizations of the Divine. Shaking has been from the beginning, and must be to the end; but now that the essentially Divine has descended into the renewed life of the human, the changes sought must be in the endeavours to bring out the deeper depths of the spiritual verities of the Divine life in the soul of man. And this endeavour must be the work, not only of the epochs of time, but likewise of all the cycles of eternity. Such efforts are necessary to enlarge, sustain, and develop the fulness of the life of God in the soul of man. And we are not to be alarmed at the apparent failures of the Church and the bitter attack of infidelity upon Christianity. These aid the birth throes of higher forms and deeper realizations of religious life. Such has been the past experience of the Church.

To endeavour to introduce the spirit of accommodation into the religious life of man, or to seek to yield the spirit and to polish the forms of religion so as to meet the cravings of self-seeking in an age of declension, is to mistake the character of Christianity, and to betray the power of the Church. Christianity can never conform itself to its surroundings, or comply with the tastes of those it came to win and to rule. It is essentially sovereign, and must ever assert its royal right to reign in the hearts and over the lives of men; and it can reign only in its true, and in no false or assumed spirit. Accommodation of Christian principles or teaching to the likings of men, with the view of retaining or reclaiming the frivolous to a

Christian profession, would be an acknowledgment of felt weakness and inherent decay. It would be the confession that Christ has not in and from Himself all that is necessary to effect all that He has undertaken to accomplish, and that He must give place to another to finish what He has begun; in other words, to give up Christianity into the hands of infidelity, the end scepticism is eagerly desirous of securing. Such a course would be suicidal. It would be to have a Christianity that would always accommodate itself to the ever-shifting tastes of man; and not a Christianity of ever fresh evolution, and of infinite depths, that speak to the immutable nature and unchanging necessities of human well-being.

We must rather seek to remove from Christianity the patchwork which well-meant but weak and erring discipleship, since the fulness of the times, has been throwing around the Person and work of Christ. We are not to seek Christ, because we eat and are filled with the loaves and fishes of His miraculous producing, neither to call fire from heaven to consume those who follow not with us; nor are we to refuse the admission of little and weak ones into the presence of the Master, because we do not see how they can be benefited by Him. We are not to betray or deny Him, and when He is arrested, mocked, and crucified, forsake Him because we cannot perceive His true method of performing His work, and in our bewilderment imagine that all is lost. We must determine to know the Truth, investigate with a keen discernment the evidence He affords us of its genuine character, and then we shall be enabled to exclaim, "My Lord and my God!"

We shall then perceive that the infinite depths, the undisclosed glories, the Divine powers that are in Christ Jesus are not to be evolved after the imaginings of our limited conception, nor in accordance with the temporary likings of imperfect man, but in accordance with the unchanging conditions of human well-being, and in a manner worthy of the manifold wisdom of God, and the vast and important ends which are being wrought out by Christ Jesus.

We must perceive that the lofty ends of human salvation are not mere escapes from hell, nor the bargaining on commercial terms with God for a desired place in heaven; that the Church's work on earth is not to impose forms of belief on the consciences of men, or to enforce the restraints of ascetism on those who know nothing of the power of religious belief. From all such the religious life of man recoils, and pants to breathe the pure atmosphere of a higher and loftier region; longs for its native liberty, and strives after the freedom wherewith Christ makes His people free, and the service that is worthy of discipleship in Jesus.

In order to our entering into this lovelier and more blissful realization of Christian life, we must perceive that this sinful state of man's present existence affords the very conditions of developing the loftiest life possible, not only to the finite spiritual being of man, but to incarnate Divinity itself; that the principle of self-sacrifice, understood and acted on, is the one great power of the most illustrious of all life, is the deepest underlying principle of the Godhead itself.

CONTENTS.

	PAGE
PREFACE	V
INTRODUCTION	1

CHAPTER I.

CHRIST'S MODE OF RECEIVING AND BESTOWING GLORY 27

CHAPTER II.

CHRIST QUALIFYING HIS DISCIPLES FOR THE RECEPTION OF HIS GLORY IN THEIR PERFORMANCE OF HIS WORK 41

CHAPTER III.

MAN'S RESPONSIBILITY IN REGARD TO DIVINE QUICKENING 63

CHAPTER IV.

THE DIVINE RE-POSSESSING ITSELF OF THE HUMAN 81

CHAPTER V.

THE TRUE AND THE FALSE OF AMBITION . 97

CHAPTER VI.

THE CHARACTER OF SELF-SACRIFICE . . 119

CHAPTER VII.

THE FOLLY OF SELFISHNESS 135

CHAPTER VIII.

THE EFFICIENT PRINCIPLE OF CHRISTIAN LIFE 147

CHAPTER IX.

IS A ONENESS OF LIFE POSSIBLE TO THE FINITE WITH THE INFINITE, AND OF THE INFINITE WITH THE FINITE? . . . 169

CHAPTER X.

IS THE PRINCIPLE OF SELF-SACRIFICE ADAPTED TO THE DEEDS OF EVERY-DAY LIFE? . . 189

CHAPTER XI.

SELF-SACRIFICE THE ONLY PRINCIPLE THAT CAN RAISE THE FALLEN 203

CHAPTER XII.

THE ADAPTATION OF THE PRINCIPLE OF SELF-SACRIFICE TO THE NECESSITIES OF HUMAN WELL-BEING 217

CHAPTER XIII.

THE DOCTRINE OF CHRIST THE ONLY TEACHING ADAPTED TO THE NATURE AND CIRCUMSTANCES OF MAN 235

CHAPTER XIV.

SELF-SACRIFICE IS THE PRINCIPLE WHICH PERVADES UNIVERSAL BEING, AND MUST EMBRACE CHRISTIAN LIFE 247

CHAPTER XV.

SUMMATION 271

CHAPTER XVI.

CONCLUSION 285

INTRODUCTION.

INTRODUCTION.

MAN lives, thinks, speaks, and believes, and in the consciousness of each of these acts has the evidence in himself of the duality of his nature, of the objective and subjective of his life. In thinking, there is the mind that thinks, and the thoughts which it thinks; in speaking, there is the person who speaks, and the words which he utters; in believing, there is the individual who believes, and the truth or falsehood which he believes.

There is an obvious distinction between the subjective and the objective, as well as an intimate relation in which the one stands to the other. A life manifests itself as it is lived, and is conscious of living as it lives. A mind cannot but think, and the thought of the mind depends upon the mind : the mind is as it thinks ; a person believes as he is inclined or compelled, and an individual speaks as he thinks when he speaks his own thoughts.

The relation between the subjective and objective is close and intimate. In finite vitality the subjective is moulded by means of its objective, and by the manner of its reception of its objective. The relation of the vital germ in the seed to the substance of the seed, to the atmosphere, to the light and heat of the sun, to the moisture and quality of the soil, is apparent in the development of the life of the seed in the plant. This relation, while close and intimate in all its bearings, is incomprehensible.

The beauty, vigour, and fertility of the plant are seen to be in exact accordance with the mode in which the germ of vitality in the seed develops its life in connection with the substance of the seed, etc. If in the growth of the plant there be the least interruption of the flow of the sap from the root, or peculiarity in the mode of the plant's reception of the air, the light, the heat, the dew, that interruption or peculiarity will cause a mark or modification in the plant which will be apparent and permanent while it continues to exist.

And so in animal life ; if in the development of the embryo in the womb, or in the growth of the young, there occur the slightest interruption in the circulation of the blood, or if there be the inhaling of impure atmosphere, the partaking of improper food, or neglect of cleanliness, then that interruption or modification of the nutrition or treatment will produce a corresponding defect in the body, which will cling to it, and be apparent in its health, while it lives on throughout the entire period of its existence.

If in the body of an animal, rational or irrational, any injury or wound occurs, the injury may be repaired, the wound healed, but the scar will remain in the body throughout the entire life, and indicate, while it continues, the locality of the injury; and the prominence of the mark will be in accordance with the degree of the injury and character of the wound. The analogy of this process in vegetable and animal life holds good in the rational and spiritual life of man, only in a far greater degree; and in the historical development of the church.

The objective of finite life is independent of the life, but the finite life is not independent of its objective, or the aliment on which it feeds, and especially is this the case with the spiritual or Divine life in man. The Infinite or Absolute is in itself the all-glorious of existence, but it is to the finite consciousness what the personal life of the individual makes it. If any finite personality makes to itself a creation of the Infinite or Divine, instead of learning from what the Infinite or Divine manifests of itself, and attempts to live according to the divine life of its own creation, instead of on the immediate manifestation which the Infinite gives of itself, then the finite life or personal consciousness cannot be elevated into communion with God, and be enabled to hold satisfying fellowship with the Divine, but must be famished, dwarfed, and degraded into a resemblance of its own creation of the Infinite or Divine. The same law ruleth the life of the church.

A disinclination in the finite, however produced, to perceive the supernatural in the natural, necessarily shuts out the finite mind from the perception of the supernatural in the natural, however clearly it may be revealed in the material, intellectual, and spiritual, and thus shuts out the reluctant finite from holding fellowship with the Infinite. The mind of man never rises above its own ideals; and so it is that the objective is ever to the subjective what the subjective makes it to itself. The Infinite as the objective of the finite, is ever in itself the same. It is, however, varied in its manifestations to the different orders of finite existence, because it manifests itself to the finite as the circumstances of the finite need, and while in these manifestations it is in itself the same, it is to each individual what he conceives or believes it to be, and similarly to the sect or church. If the Church, in her incrustation of Divine manifestation in doctrine, alters in the least the aspect of that manifestation, then does she shut herself up to the necessity of contemplating God through the medium of that distortion of Divine revelation; *i.e.*, to look upon God in a false light.

If the Infinite is to be known by the finite, the Infinite must reveal Himself to the finite, and the revelation which the Infinite affords of Himself to the finite must be such a manifestation as is adapted to the condition or circumstances of the finite to which the Infinite reveals Himself. And the finite will become acquainted with or know the Infinite just as its subjective assimilates itself into a oneness with the Infinite, through its reception of and feeding upon the manifestation the Infinite affords of Himself to the finite. It is the same with the sect or church.

If there be in the finite a disinclination to receive the manifestation which the Infinite affords of Himself; then in order to the finite's coming to the reception and understanding of the manifestation which the Infinite gives to it of Himself, there must be such an operation of the Infinite on the finite as will remove the disinclination of the finite, and awake in its stead sympathy with the manifestation, and a desire to know it; in other words, there must be such a bearing of the Infinite on the subjective of the finite as will overcome its disinclination, and secure in the room of this disinclination a readiness to receive and to appreciate the afforded manifestation. It is the same with the denomination or church.

Hence, in the recovery of man, the work of the Son manifesting the Father to the world must be succeeded by the work of the Spirit removing the disinclination of the carnal mind by the quickening of the soul of man with the sympathy and love of the Divine, as He takes the things which are Christ's, and shows them unto the awaking spirit of faith or belief. The Spirit awakes faith in the waiters upon God, as He reveals to the inner eye of the soul the manifestations which God has given of Himself to man in His Son. And in all these manifestations and operations of His grace God never interferes with the free agency of man, or tampers in the least with the principles, laws, or ends of being, but acts in perfect accordance with the functions of all finite life, and the ecclesiastical condition of His church.

These are facts which ought to be patent to every intelligent mind. The varied conditions of men on earth in connection with God's grace are not at variance or inconsistent with the principles of God's dealings with any or all of His creatures; could we penetrate into the inner depths of the Divine essence, we would see that these had all their source there, and were all in accordance with His wisdom, and worthy of Him. We cannot, while in this life, perceive all the relations of the principles, powers, and operations of God's grace; we cannot discern them in their modes of working and methods of securing their ends. These, do what we may to comprehend them, lie for the present beyond our penetration. Secret things belong to the Lord our God; but the things which are revealed, unto us and to our children for ever, that we may do all the will of the Lord in our private life and public work.

Our imperative duty is to ask God's Spirit, that He may incline our hearts to keep His law. It is incumbent on us to study God's truth, to walk in accordance with His will, whether that will is expressed in the indications of nature, the precepts of revelation, or the gracious manifestations of His Spirit in the soul; and thus to yield our hearts up to God's awakening in them the rising of the Divine. By whatever means or methods we can learn the indications of God's will, it is our duty to acquire that knowledge, and to obey it in our thoughts, feelings, and deeds of life.

Transmission is necessary to fellowship. Without interchange there can be no communion, and the necessity of fellowship between the Infinite and the finite is that the Infinite come into the finite in the creation of capacity or sympathy, and disclose Himself to this capacity as it is able to receive His manifestations. The finite, in order to its assimilation and expansion by means of its reception of the Divine, must steadily contemplate, conform to, and cordially enjoy its reception of the Divine. This is true of the individual and of the church.

If the human mind does not receive the exact impression from the objective, if it learns not from the pages of creation and revelation, the thoughts of God as expressed in these pages,—if its conception of the nature and end of being be not the same as the Divine,—then it possesses not truth, its subjective is not one with its objective, it enjoys not communion with the Divine, but is in disunion and conflict with God.

This disunion and conflict with the Divine may result from confusion either in the objective or the subjective of human life, *i.e.*, either from confusion in the work of God—the pages of revelation, or from conflict in the nature of man —disease in the organ of human vision. This confusion, either in the reader or in the pages read, cannot reach the principles revealed. Man, however confused or conflicting in his views, feels himself shut up to certain elementary principles of belief.

And the necessity of agreeable fellowship between the immaculately pure Jehovah and His sinful creature man, is that God comes near and into the guilty spirit of the fallen, in such a manifestation of His love and purpose as will remove the consciousness of guilt from the soul by filling the heart with loyal affection; and as He thus works in the inner nature or heart of man, God produces the faith of His gracious purpose, destroys the consciousness of rebelliousness, and awakes felt delight and satisfaction in complying with the Father's will in the individual and in the church.

And thus, in order to the renewal of fellowship between God and man, God through His self-sacrificing grace must recreate the chaos of the carnal into the devotedness of the filial; and the human, in and by believing, must yield itself up to the reconciling of the Divine, so that beholding as in a glass the glory of the Lord, he may be changed into the same image, from glory to glory, by the Spirit of the Lord.

As the Absolute must come into the conditioned or self-sacrificing to disclose Himself to the finite, so the human must rise out of the carnal into the consciousness of the self-sacrificing, ere man can realize fellowship with God in the highest manifestations of the Divine. While man remains in the consciousness of the carnal, the visions of the glory of the Infinite in the self-sacrificing of the Divine are to him as impossible as would be the clear perception of the loveliness of nature to him who has a film covering his eyes. Realization of fellowship with God in the bliss of self-sacrifice is to the carnal mind an utter impossibility.

It is only in the progressive discernment of the True, and in the enlarging fellowship of the Divine, that the possible of human capacity can be realized. Every feeling of aversion in the spirit, every phase of error in the mind, every perversion of love in the heart, every movement of self in the soul of man against the Divine, is a loss and an evil to the human which the Infinite alone can perceive, and for which no possible attainment and enjoyment of the finite can make up. As a mind cannot realize the benefit and delight of a perception in advance of or out of the reach of its intellectual discernment; so the heart cannot know the benefit and joy of a vision of the Divine beyond the degree of the purity of its love or the measure of its devotion to God; and so with the church.

It is only in the grace of self-sacrificing love that the Godhead can disclose its radiant brightness, and it is only in the grateful admiration and delight of the filial heart in the conscious sacrifice of the self of the carnal, that the human can enter into and comprehend the breadth and length, the depth and height, and know the love of Christ which passeth knowledge, and be filled with all the fulness of God. The paramount duty and the chief interest of the sinner is not to be concerned about escaping from hell;

nor does it lie in acrimonious discussions, eager inquiries about abstractions, and doctrines which lie beyond the ken of mortals. But it is yielding up his heart to the striving Spirit of God, to realize the faith which enables him to know the truth as it is in Jesus.

The carnal can never desire or labour with eagerness to destroy itself. This in the very nature of things is an impossibility. The selfish can only be subdued by the overcoming love of the self-sacrificing; the rebel sentiment of self-will can be expelled from the spirit only by the invading light of loyalty; the insensibility of the carnal can be removed only by the quickening of the Divine. This law holds good in the church, as well as in the individual soul.

God in Himself is ever one and the same— the absolutely perfect, all-glorious, and ever-blessed One; His manifestations are worthy of Him, and in themselves are the same and equal to all; yet they are to His creatures what each of them makes them to be. Each one will conceive of these manifestations as he is inclined. Inclination, or the subjective condition of the creature, is the medium and means of its true greatness or degradation, of its bliss or woe. The nature or constitution of a creature determines its capacity or position in the scale of existence, and its inclination corresponds with its nature.

The jelly speck of protoplasm in the womb contains in it the possibility of the finest physical frame that ever appeared on earth, the natural embodiment of the loftiest intellect that ever scanned the works of God, the divinest spirit ever indwelt by God; and yet, as the tiny film of the spider spun round the rosebud will prevent its outburst into blossom, so the insignificant inclination of the carnal mind may frustrate man's realization of his lofty destiny.

While a creature gifted with a capacity to rise to the loftiest condition of glory and bliss —notwithstanding all the influences acting on him to lift him up—resists all the powers brought to operate constitutionally on him, refuses to co-operate with the agencies urging him to comply, as they awake within the beginning of a new life, shuts his inner eye, resists the constraining power of Divine manifestations given to raise him, he must come short of the realization and enjoyment of the Divine life. If all the adaptation, freeness, and riches of God's grace fail to move him, then, notwithstanding all the possibility of nature and capability of circumstance, he will not rise out of his degradation and woe to the true condition of his well-being.

And as it is in the beginning, so is it with the progress of the work of grace in the soul of man, and the attainment of its reward. As the human capacity receives, so it is filled with all the fulness of God; as the germ of the Divine life in the soul unfolds itself through his working out what the Spirit works in him to will and to do, so the Spirit of God dwells in and manifests Himself to the spirit of the believer. As the life of the believer develops itself in feeding on the pure and unadulterated Bread of Life, so the soul assimilates to the image of

God's Son. The same holds good in the sect, denomination, and church. If the life of the spirit of man receive not the pure truth of the Word in the love of it, then the spirit of man realizes not the pure life of God. If in any way the spirit of man refuses to conform to the Spirit of God in the development of its life, it may recover from its lapse, but it will carry with it the mark of its mishap, or the scar of its wound, and realize the consciousness of its disaster throughout its after-existence.

The Father is in the Son and by the Spirit. The unconditioned, self-sufficing, infinite, and eternal God conditions Himself, not merely in the Creator, Preserver, Ruler, Judge, Avenger, but above all in the Father. These are but lower stages of His manifestations. Father sums up the conditionings of the absolute. God is under no necessity of conditioning Himself, or of coming under limitations, but being pleased to do so, He has no other form that can adequately express the relations He is pleased to form with man, than that of Father.

The Father reveals Himself in the Son, who, being the express image of His Person, or the conditioned form of the invisible God, the Logos, in whom it pleased the Father that all fulness should dwell, in whom are hid all the treasures of wisdom and knowledge, in whom dwells the fulness of the Godhead bodily, is the ladder of the Father's descent, and of the believer's ascent.

The Son imparts Himself consciously to the believer in a oneness of spirit. Man, in ceasing to resist by yielding himself up to the in-breathing of the one Spirit, becomes one in spirit, mind, and life, with God's own Son. As he drinks in the one Spirit, he is one in the spiritual with God's own Son, one in the consciousness of Divine life, one in the realization of glory and joy; and it is only as he becomes one in spirit with the Son of God that he can enter into the spiritual of being, live the life of God, realize the glory and bliss of existence, have access into the presence or fellowship of the Father—know God.

This is the mystery of revelation and faith. In the manifestation of Himself, the Absolute comes into or under the condition of revelation, discloses Himself in a series of out-comings—descends into the fulness of the times; and man by faith sees the Invisible, ascends into the heights of the Divine, assimilates into the likeness of God's own Son. In this process there is illimitable capacity of becoming filled with boundless fulness. The Absolute coming under conditions that the finite may rise out of the limitation of evil into the boundless fellowship of the Divine; the Absolute conditioning Himself in the condescending love of self-sacrifice to the necessities of the ascent of man out of the carnal or selfish;—this is the glorious and blessed mystery which is being disclosed to the visions of faith in the consciousness of the life divine.

The Christianity which makes known to the world a spirit which is so different as to be the very opposite of what it cherishes; which is the only power of man's well-being, and which for its embrace requires the greatest possible self-denial; which is so opposite to all the radical elements of all human religions, as to require the expulsion of those elements from the minds of those believing in Jesus; the reception of which necessitates the expulsion of man's natural conception regarding God, and his relations to Him, and of his conception of God's disposition to man, may be seen at a glance to be a religion which makes such a demand of man, and produces such a result in him, as renders it impossible that it should be of man.

Christ, however, is original, not merely in the one characteristic of self-sacrifice, but in all that is peculiar to Him,—in His working, His work, His tuition, His philosophy, indeed, in the whole of His being and doing. There is not *one* lineament of His graceful portraiture to be met with in equal perfection in all the prior thinking of the Jew or Gentile in the eastern or western world. Nor in them can we find one fragment of that conception of His work, the striking characteristic of which is the raising through His own self-sacrifice the chief of sinners to be the very chief of saints, the conferring of His highest honours on His most malicious blasphemer, the employing in His noblest service His bitterest foe. Nor is there one shred of that tuition, the marked peculiarity of which is that there is greater joy among the innocent and loyal spirits of glory over the repentance of one sinner, than over vast numbers of just and virtuous persons. Nor is there the dimmest apprehension in the speculations of the sages of the philosophy which lays bare the profound truth that the affection of the much-pardoned far outmeasures in depth, tenderness, and purity the love of the unfallen, and thus opens their illimitable capacities for the inflowing of that love which affords to them the comprehension of the incomprehensible, so as to be filled with all the fulness of God. This philosophy, contemplated in the presence of the ethical teaching of the Gentile and self-righteous doctrine of the Jew, is of itself sufficient to demonstrate the unearthly character of Christ's mode of viewing life in its relations and possibilities.

Although in a somewhat different form, we may sum up the subject-matter of the following pages thus: Man is an ambitious being, he is so by the deep, indestructible instinct of his soul, and by the fervently cherished sentiments of his heart.

Man actuated by selfish ambition has performed wonderful deeds, displayed amazing powers, attained to widespread fame, but only to his own disappointment and the injury of others.

Man actuated by the spirit of self-sacrificing ambition has accomplished the most stupendous work that has been or ever will be performed in time or eternity, has lived the most illustrious life, secured the greatest benefit to humanity that has been or ever will be possible in time or eternity, has formed the loveliest character that has or ever will be known in present or future ages, has, in yielding to the sufferings of moments, realized the purest, most satisfying, and enduring bliss, won the brightest glory, and founded an everlasting empire.

This world of sin is probably the only sphere in all God's universe, where man by ambitious self-sacrifice can achieve a marvellous work, acquire a glorious character, lay the basis of the sweetest and most enduring bliss.

In the invitation of the great and glorious Self-sacrificer, men are called by God to the performance of a great work—to the acquisition of a pure and bright glory—to the realization of a deep, enduring, and satisfying bliss.

Why is it that the Christian Church in the nineteenth century of her existence is not in the enjoyment of her millennial glory and bliss? simply and only because she has not recognised and realized the grandeur, importance, and power of the principle of self-sacrifice.

And how comes it that of all the ambitious and covetous men that have ever appeared on the earth, and striven to immortalize themselves by the performance of stupendous deeds, the humble Nazarene is the only man who has perceived and exemplified the power of self-sacrificing ambition, and by so doing draws the world into the imitation of Himself in His wondrous life and death?—into the ascent with Him to the realization of universal and ever-enduring empire over all evil, in the enjoyment of endless bliss and satisfying joy?

Self-sacrifice is the outcome of the inmost perfection of Godhead, and could have been known in its highest perfection and manifested in its fullest power only by the Incarnate One.

I.

CHRIST'S MODE OF RECEIVING AND BESTOWING GLORY.

CHAPTER I.

CHRIST'S MODE OF RECEIVING AND BESTOWING GLORY.

MAN thirsts for glory, and strives after its possession in many ways; but he perceives not the superiority of inner to outer possessions, or of spiritual to material glory; and thus it is that he fails of acquiring true greatness, and of obtaining enduring possessions. The idea of Christianity being a mere deliverance, a sociality, a philosophy, and a kingdom of peace, is inadequate to the true life of God in the soul of man. The Church of Christ is the arena of a protracted warfare, a mighty conflict, and a sublime victory. The controversy between Satan and Christ is regarding the agency and method of establishing the kingdom of heaven, or the reign of glorious life on earth: whether it shall be by self-gratification or self-sacrifice. In the one method the disciple realizes a momentary and superficial enjoyment, with deep and enduring distress; in the other a momentary and superficial distress, with a deep and enduring enjoyment.

Every disciple of Jesus is a soldier fighting for his Lord, in winning his immortal crown. Christian life is not simply an obligation or service, but a privilege and opportunity, an enviable grace to be seized and delighted in. Until it is regarded as more than an obligation or a service, and is looked upon as an opportunity of acquiring glory in the display of true heroism, of self-sacrifice, its real consciousness will not be realized, nor its exalted character displayed. The non-perception of this is the explanation of so much formality and selfishness in the self-sacrificing Church of the self-sacrificing One, and of so much devotion and service to the world.

The combination of inherent and acquired greatness is the perfection of moral character. The inherent is necessary to the acquired. The tree bears fruit in accordance with its nature. The life lived is fashioned after its radical principle. The character formed is in accordance with the motive, principle, and aim of life. The sinner, in order to live the true life of man upon earth, or form the real Christian character in time, must yield himself up to the quickening Spirit of the living God, and by working out what the Spirit works in him to will and to do, put on the Lord Jesus.

To win His glory, form His wonderful character, accomplish His gracious work, Christ had to become incarnate—His human had to be indwelt by His Divine nature. To acquire glory in a sinful world (the true sphere of winning glory), two things are necessary—the Divine working on and dwelling in the human, and the human working out what the Divine works in it, to will and to do, in accordance with individual circumstances.

God gives to man both directly and indirectly; He gives directly in order to His giving indirectly; *i.e.*, He must first give directly, ere the receiver can acquire what He gives indirectly. In other words, man must act in accordance with what he has received directly from God, ere God will give to him indirectly. God gives indirectly through man's acting in accordance with what He has already given him directly. God gives glory to man through his acting in accordance with his renewed nature and circumstances. Glory is the radiance of matter, the brilliance of illustrious deeds, the true nobility of heroic character. Glory is essential and acquired. Essential glory cannot be won, acquired glory must. It is not of His essential glory that

Christ speaks when, addressing His Father, He says, "The glory Thou hast given me I have given them," but of His acquired glory, the glory He won as the servant of His Father, in His self-sacrificing encounter with, and overcoming of, the powers and principalities of evil; and this is the glory Christ shares with His disciples in the measure of their self-sacrificing imitation of Him.

Christ received glory from God in receiving from Him His appointment, His qualifications, the circumstances in which He wrought, and the reward of His working.

Christ received His appointment from His Father in humility, in love, in ardent devotion to the glory of God and the good of men. No pride, arrogance, or vanity, ever characterized the life or actions of Jesus of Nazareth. He ever realized and cherished the feeling of dependence upon His Father. He saw what was with His Father, and learned from Him. He spake and only spake the words He learned from His Father, He did and only did the deeds He saw with His Father; and thus He could say, The words which I speak, and the deeds which I do, are not mine, but the Father's, which sent me.

Christ accepted of the qualifications for His

work from His Father; He descended into the "holy thing" which was prepared for His indwelling in the womb of the Virgin. He lived among sinful men, in the presence of His Father, ever feeding His ardent zeal by spending nights of inspiring commune with His Father; and thus He received the unmeasured fulness of the indwelling Spirit of His Father. This was the manner in which He qualified Himself for the performance of the work His Father gave Him to do.

Christ received from His Father the circumstances in which He wrought. He accepted of His life in a sinful world; of His encounter with the spirits of darkness; of His sufferings from the hands of sinful men as instigated by demons; of the anguish of His spirit in His encounter with Satan; of the hiding of His Father's face as He hung in agony on the cross. It was no matter of surprise to Him that He was led up of the Spirit into the wilderness, to be tempted of the devil; neither was He taken unawares when He was assailed by the artifice of cruel and wicked men; nor was He amazed that He was left by His Father to the full fury of the deadly rage of the devil. He knew that it was only thus that He could display the power of the Divine in the human in a sinful world, and allure men to the imitation of His self-sacrifice. And thus it may be seen that if Christ had not come and done what He did, by the appointment of His Father, in this sinful world, His character would not have been so glorious.

Christ did not murmur at the opposition He had to encounter. He knew that ore, to be made available, had to be smelted; that marble, to assume the beautiful figure of man, had to pass under the chisel of the sculptor; that gold, to ornament the neck of beauty, required to be shapen by the skill of the artificer; that the diamond, to appear in its brightness, had to be polished by the hand of the lapidary; that the student, to acquire knowledge, had to devote himself to the study of nature and the reading of books; that the warrior, to win his crown, had to contend successfully in the fight; and that even He, to acquire His glory, had to pass through all that was necessary for His appearance in its pure radiance.

Hence Christ did not shrink from His undertaking, nor strive to alter in the least the conditions under which He had to work, but nerved Himself for the successful discharge of His duties by continual communings with His Father. He did not fret, murmur, or repine at what befell Him, or fold His arms in dread or dismay, and long to be away from the scene of toil and suffering. He did not regret that He had undertaken His work, and wish that He had never come into this world of sin. While keenly alive to all He had to encounter, He set Himself with devotion to the accomplishment of His task. He knew the value of life in a sinful world, the precious opportunities of doing good in the sphere of self-sacrifice, the fleeting character of time, and the importance of seizing its every moment. Hence He braced His spirit by meditation and prayer, He aroused His soul by cherishing ardent love to God and man, and fired His zeal by the steady contemplation of the joy that was set before Him. And thus if Christ had not encountered and overcome the opposition He met with, His character would not have been so glorious.

Christ understood His work. He asked and received from His Father the Spirit necessary for its accomplishment. He never complained of the work His Father had given Him to do. He knew that motive characterizes action, that devotion to duty beautifies character and life, that perseverance secures success. Nor did He wish that His surroundings had been different from what He found them. He did not loathe the wicked, scorn their presence, and long for other and better society. While hating sin, and grieving over its power in the sinner, He pitied him in his wretchedness and guilt, longed for his emancipation, strove to win him to purity of life and loftiness of character by displaying before him the loveliness of Divine patience, meekness, and long-suffering in bearing with the contradiction of sinners against Himself. He did not desire an easier way of accomplishing His work, nor did He engage in it in a mercenary spirit; He cherished ardent love to His work, and breathed the spirit of true devotion into His undertaking, and He gave Himself in self-sacrifice to its performance; and He did so because He saw into the nature of being, the principles of life, and the character of glory and joy. Christ knew what was the consciousness of doing and of having done the illustrious. He was aware of what was the satisfaction of having toiled and suffered in the accomplishment of the illustrious. He realized the joy of seeing the fruit of His illustrious deeds. Hence, if Christ had not performed His work in the spirit in which He accomplished it, His character would not have been so glorious, nor His joy so pure.

Christ toiled not only to acquire glory from His Father for Himself, but that He might manifest it to men, and allure them into the quest and reception of it from Himself.

If men are to receive of the glory which Christ gives to His disciples from His Father, they must accept of His appointment to the work which He gives them to do, and accept of it in humble dependence on Him, in love to God and man, and in ardent devotion to the glory of His kingdom. They must also accept of their qualifications from Him for the performance of the work He gives them to do. They must be quickened with His life, live in His presence, be filled with His spirit. They must also accept of the circumstances in which He calls them to work in this sinful world, of their encounter with the spirits of temptation, and of their suffering from the hands of men and devils; nor may they murmur at the opposition they have to meet, nor repine at the difficulties they have to encounter. They are to remember that trials and conflicts are necessary to discipline, and that skilful energy in the conflict alone can secure victory and the enjoyment of it. Neither may they strive to alter the circumstances in which Christ places them, nor fret over what befalls them, nor fold their arms in regret, longing to be away from this world of sin, and wishing they had never engaged in Christian work. They must brace their spirits by meditation and prayer, fire their souls by cherishing ardent zeal for the glory of their Master, and animate their minds by the contemplation of the joy that is set before them.

And they are to work in Christ's spirit, ever bearing in mind that motive characterizes action, that devotion beautifies character and life, and that perseverance leads to success. They are not to loathe contact with the wicked, nor long to be in better society, but ever to keep steadfastly in mind that it is only among the sinful that they can work Christ's work. Nor are they to seek for easier methods of effecting the work which He gives them to do. They are not to engage in Christ's work in a selfish or mercenary spirit, but are to breathe into it the ardour of love and self-sacrifice, knowing that they can accomplish it only in self-sacrificing devotion to the glory of God and the good of man.

This aspect of Christ's receiving and imparting glory, while spread before the view of the Church for nearly nineteen centuries, has hardly yet been discerned by it. The apostles had a vision of it, but it cost them a hard struggle and a special training to attain to it; they did not easily and of themselves learn the contrast between heavenly and earthly sovereignty. The sovereigns of the world come forth in great pomp and pageantry, to feed their vanity and empty conceit by receiving the homage of fawning and flattering myriads; but the Sovereign of the Universe came forth from the "most excellent glory" into the society of men in meekness and humility, not to be ministered unto, but to minister unto the wants of sinful humanity, by scattering in rich profusion the gifts of infinite love, and to lay down His life that He might rescue sinners from their selfishness, and restore them in filial love to God.

What then is the end to which Christianity directs the eye of man? Escape from dreaded ruin, deliverance from all evil, introduction into the enjoyment of boundless fulness, a position among the greatest and most illustrious of all times and of all regions, visions of dazzling glory and of rapturous bliss, likeness to God, appearing among the manifested sons of the Highest in the fulness of power, in the sweetness of uninterrupted fellowship with the Father, Son, and Spirit, in the gracious reign over all. Yes, to all these; but in what and how? Not in the physical, the social, the rational, the speculative, and selfish, but in the spiritual, the self-sacrificing, the divine.

What is the real foundation of fellowship with Christ in His reign of glory and bliss? His work for us? Yes. And what is the true qualification for appearing with Christ in His glory and bliss? is it our wealth? our power? our standing in society? our fame in this life? our attainments in the arts, sciences, philosophy, literature? our ecclesiastical deeds? Ah, no. It is our conscious oneness with Christ in nature, life, and work; our fellowship with Him in the spiritual and divine; our imitation of Him in His self-denying devotion to the re-quickening of the human with the life of God; participation with Him in His stooping to be raised on the cross, where in the ardour of His self-sacrificing love He exclaimed, " Father, forgive them, for they know not what they do." In the consciousness of the faintest approach to this spirit in life and death, is the true qualification for appearing with Him in His glory.

If we are to appear with Christ in His glory, we must receive our appointments and qualifications from Him for the performance of His work; act in His spirit, and for His glory. If we do not receive our appointment and qualification from Him, we cannot do His work; and if we receive our appointment and qualification from Him, yet fail to act in His spirit, and for His glory, we cannot win His approbation, nor appear with Him in His glory.

II.

CHRIST'S QUALIFYING HIS DISCIPLES FOR THE RECEPTION OF HIS GLORY, IN THEIR PERFORMANCE OF HIS WORK.

CHAPTER II.

CHRIST'S QUALIFYING HIS DISCIPLES FOR THE RECEPTION OF HIS GLORY, IN THEIR PERFORMANCE OF HIS WORK.

MAN by an instinct of his nature desires to be religious, but by the force of depravity is eager to content himself with the least possible amount of spiritual life. He is more taken up with the formal than the vital—the ritual and ceremonial than the intellectual and gracious of religious communion with God. He would be religious rather in the selfish than in the self-sacrificing. This is exhibited in the experience of the apostles in connection with the method and labour of Christ in training them to embrace the life of self-sacrifice.

Man is unfit in himself for receiving the glory of Christ—not in capacity or circumstance, but because of his religious prejudices and selfishness. The disciples were a striking illustration of this fact. What could the "twelve" make of Christ's declaration to His Father in their hearing, "The glory which Thou gavest me I have given them"? Why could they not understand these words? They had every possible religious advantage men could have possessed. But instead of employing their advantages to the rooting out of their prejudices, they used them to feed their selfishness.

Christ's difficulty with His disciples was the same as it is with all imperfect religious men, *i.e.*, to rend the veil of their prejudice, and to induce them to see His truth in its own light, that they might enter into the inner fellowship of His love. But as yet they had no sympathy with the essentials of Christian life, and hence they had to pass through a severe ordeal, ere they could, through listening to the still small voice, enter into the fellowship of self-sacrifice. And the hindrance they had to overcome was in their selfish prejudice, and not in the spirit of heroic martyrdom.

The disciples had dreamed of realizing the supreme of life in the Jewish, the politico-ecclesiastical, the ritual, the formal, the devotional of fellowship with the Messiah, and expected to find their entire satisfaction in such forms of religious life, but they met only with disappointment, as all must who entertain similar conceptions and make the same attempt. They had a vague conscious craving, a longing after a fuller and more satisfying condition of life, and hence they were eager that their Master should set up His kingdom, and assign to them their respective places in it; but they were wholly ignorant of the sublime place of self-sacrifice, and of how they were to enter upon the purer and loftier enjoyments of the Messianic reign. They were somewhat willing to extend the benefits of the Messiah's kingdom to the Gentiles, on the condition of their becoming Jews; but that all who were to enter into the enjoyment of spiritual life in Christ Jesus should possess themselves of their positions in the kingdom of the Messiah, on the same principle of self-sacrifice as that by which Christ Himself won His glory, never entered into their minds. The light of such illumination could not penetrate the dark chasm of their prejudice. Of this higher, sublime, and more enduring realm of light, love and self-sacrifice, they had not the most distant conception; such a region of spiritual life was to them far out of sight.

And to receive them into this realm of light and life was the object of Christ's return to them from the invisible world. It was not to take them out of this world of sin into some other region of space, where they might enjoy repose and enjoyment to their hearts' content, but to introduce them into a new condition of life on earth, a new medium of fellowship with the seen and temporal, by means of new conceptions of the unseen and eternal,—into a life of new motives, principles, and ends, of living in the only sphere where such life could be realized—a life the very opposite of what they had coveted and eagerly desired to possess. They had sought to live in the realm of selfishness, striving after the chief places, powers, and honours, in dreams of triumph over the Gentiles, whom they were to subdue and govern. They had delighted in their fancied conceit of being beyond all other men the favourites of Heaven. Hence they were appalled at the arrest, condemnation, and death of their Master, the very thing which was necessary to break in upon their prejudice, and prepare them for clearer light. They were not only appalled, but disappointed, bewildered, and stunned, so confounded as to be unable to realize the fact of His resurrection.

But having suffered the shock which was fitted to drive them out of all their fondly cherished dreams of a political Messiah, a theocratic kingdom, Christ returned to them from the tomb, that He might receive them into purer regions, of fuller fellowship with Himself, into a life to be realized in the discernment of the spiritual and divine of man's nature and opportunities, a life to be known in the entire consecration of their being and doing to the highest good of all. They were now to live in the constant view of humanity being the image of God—of man's glory in being indwelt by the Divine—of the necessity of expelling the insane, self-tormenting dream of selfishness from the human breast, by the quickening of the soul of man with the Spirit of Christ. They were to become conscious of the unparalleled grandeur of effecting the transformation from the selfish to the self-sacrificing, and of expelling the devilish by the renewing with the Divine; especially when this was achieved through a momentary realization of obscurity and suffering.

Christ's return to His disciples had to correspond with His departure from them. It was not a mere return in space, but in the fuller disclosure of Himself to them, that He might raise them into a conscious oneness of life with Himself. His return to them was an entrance into their understandings, lives, aspirations, zeal, and consciousness, that they might be lifted into the apprehension and realization of His. He came to them to change their conceptions of the character of His kingdom and reign, that they might become qualified for sharing His glory and joy. He came to them as the Conqueror of all evil, the Consecrator of all power in heaven and earth to the reign of love and peace. He appeared before them as the glorious Self-sacrificer, who could be known only by conscious sympathy with Him in His self-sacrificing. Thus they recognized, but did not know Him; He was the same in Himself, yet very different to them. Hence He required to afford them infallible proofs of His resurrection. Yet in the presence of what should have overwhelmed them with evidence they doubted. And of these infallible proofs they of all men were the most competent to judge. In regard to such evidence it was impossible that they could have been deceived. Of the identity of His Person He afforded them the most indubitable evidence it was possible for them to receive or for Him to afford. He appeared in their presence, not once, but frequently; they saw Him, they heard Him, they conversed with Him, "they handled Him with their hands," they ate with Him, they drank with Him, they journeyed with Him; He showed them His hands and His feet, and in them the prints of the nails, and in His side the mark of the spear. They were familiar with His voice and the manner of His address. He talked and conversed with them, and the subject-matter of His conversation was so peculiar in its character, that they could not but have recognized its identity.

He not only afforded them the clearest evidence possible to their bodily senses, but likewise the most forcible proofs possible to their intellectual powers and spiritual perceptions. His manner of intercourse with them was so characteristic of Him, that they could not have mistaken another for Him. To those who met Him by His own appointment on the mountain of Galilee, He displayed the same extraordinary powers which He had been in the habit of manifesting while He was with them alive. His appearance, His discourse, the matter and manner of His instructions, were the same after His resurrection that they had been before His death. The doctrines He taught them, the promises He made them, the work He assigned them, the signs He showed them were the very things He had so frequently spoken of, that they could not have mistaken either the speaker or the subject of His address. These were not only so peculiar to Him, but so different, nay, so opposite to anything they had ever heard from any other, that deception in the matter was an absolute impossibility. Why then were they not fully convinced, and ready to embrace His doctrines, and engage in His mission? because of the inveteracy of their prejudices regarding a political Messiah, and the difficulty they felt in casting aside their Jewish notions. It required the cumulative influence of the "forty days'" teaching, and the descent of the Holy Ghost, not only in "cloven tongues," but in fulness of His renewing grace, to raise them into a conscious oneness with Christ regarding His mission and the method of prosecuting it.

Christ came from the bosom of bliss into this world of sin on the embassy of mercy to a fallen race. He came into the nature and responsibilities of man, that He might encounter and overcome the principalities of evil, by enduring their inveterate hate, in the display of the loftiest self-sacrifice, for an example to His followers. In this He displayed the tenderness of His own and His Father's love, the graciousness of the Divine purpose to a sinful world. We have only to study the manner of Christ's meeting with His disciples, and the mode of His intercourse with them during the "forty days" after His resurrection, to perceive how hard it was for the apostles to rise above their prejudices, and to be struck with the love and tenderness which characterised His intercourse with them, and the earnestness of His purpose to raise them to the discernment of the Divine of self-sacrifice.

Love hastened Him into their midst. He felt for their disconsolate condition, and was anxious to give them correct views of the purpose of His death. The treatment He received from them in no way cooled, but rather intensified, the ardour of His love. His immediate return to them was not only a clear proof of His love, but also of the nature of His mission and of the wisdom with which he had trained them for their work. The manner in which He met His disciples, and conducted Himself towards them, is a beautiful illustration of the benignity and tenderness of His love, and was well calculated to afford them a glimpse of His self-sacrificing character. His address to Mary Magdalene, His conversation with the two disciples, His intercourse with Thomas, and His treatment of Peter; in short, His whole dealings with the eleven, were designed and fitted to prepare them for the descent of the Spirit.

And hence He came to them not only *in* but *for* love; not merely to embrace them in His affection, but to enable them to realize it in their hearts, and to kindle in their spirits the same flame that glowed in His own. Herein lies the depths of man's existence, of his redemption and of his glorious life. Man realizes his existence only as he lives in love, the love in which God realizes His being and life. Hence man is near to God, nay, identified with Him, not in the consciousness of an underived existence, but in the consciousness of a love realizing itself in the sacrifice of itself for the benefit of its objects. What a capacity for love is there in man! what a deliverance from the enmity of selfishness is there in Christ! what a glorious Divine life is held out for humanity in the consciousness of self-sacrificing devotedness to the cause of God in man! It is a being filled with all the fulness of God, when the heart of man glows with the very same self-sacrificing love which glows in the heart of God Himself. What a security, dignity, glory, and bliss to be bound to God with the most powerful, assimilating, sweetest bond of all possible ties! He that dwelleth in love dwelleth in God, and God in him. Love is a blissful condition of life; it fills the soul of the lover (in the measure of his love) with the bliss of life. The love of God, with all the fulness of His life, is the highest possible life, the most satisfying condition of conceivable existence.

Christ returned to His disciples in the manifestation of His grace to fire their spirits with the zeal of self-sacrifice. This was the necessary accompaniment of His return to them in love. He came to them, not only with the full forgiveness of all their past delinquencies, but to take occasion from such to raise them in fuller measure into the consciousness of His own higher life. He can return to any of His disciples only in a higher measure of grace; He came to them not only to display but to impart to them this grace, nor solely to make them conscious of its reign in their inner being, but that they might likewise display it in their outer lives. He manifested Himself to them that He might draw them out of their false conception of Him and His kingdom, into correct knowledge of the end for which He displayed His self-sacrificing grace. He returned to them that He might allure them into the zeal of winning His as He had won His Father's glory; to draw them into the perception of the true grandeur and dignity of the human spirit in itself, and of the honour and glory of its becoming all engrossed with the conception of consecrating life to the work of raising immortal souls from the bondage of the demon spirit of self-conceit into the realization of true human greatness through conscious fellowship with the Godhead in its self-sacrifice on behalf of man. And it required all His desire and deeds to secure His end with them.

Christ returned to His disciples to open their understandings to a clear discernment of the principles of His kingdom and reign. Before His death, in the face of all His teaching to the contrary, they would cling to their own conceptions of the world-wide kingdom their Master was by the sword about to establish on earth, in subjugating the Gentile to the Jew. They had often dreamed of the powers they were to wield, nay, contended among themselves about the chief places they were to occupy in it, and the glory they should enjoy, when they should sit with Him as His councillors of state. So engrossed were their hearts with such conceits, that notwithstanding His many efforts to bring them to right conceptions, His exertions were all fruitless. Their prejudices so far closed their minds against His endeavours, that His death was necessary to stun and overwhelm them. Now that they had so far recovered from that shock, and were satisfied of the reality of His resurrection, they listened to His discourses, with minds shattered in prejudice, and hearts opening to the drawing of His truth, so that they could apprehend something of the self-sacrificing character of His work, and of the spirituality of His reign.

He thus drew them into a dawning apprehension of the glorious nature and results of His passing through an anguish of bloody sweat, to a death of desertion on the cross of infamy, for the reclamation of a murderous world to the perception of the wondrous character, and to the admiration of the Divine nature, of self-sacrifice. But for the clear and full vision of the radiant glory of such, and for the ready giving up of themselves to entire conformity with Him in this one characteristic of His being and doing, they had to wait till they were endued with the Spirit from on high. It was only then that they could rise to the sublime height of glorying in the cross of Christ; then they could see His glory, covet earnestly the better gifts, pursue the more excellent way; then they could face a frowning world, if only by expelling the enmity of the carnal from the spirits of men they could win sinners to God, and thus become the instruments of transforming demons into seraphs. In thus extending Christ's kingdom they would sit with Him in His high council, reign with Him in swaying the sceptre of His power, and open wide the floodgates of everlasting bliss in immortal souls.

As the "eleven" were "endued with the Spirit from on high," they began to perceive something of the vast and enduring kingdom Christ had won by His self-sacrifice, and realized in His conscious victory of the Divine, a kingdom founded on very different, nay, opposite principles from those of which they had dreamed, and which rule in the political states of earth; a kingdom fashioned by a far higher vitality than that which builds up the rich and beautiful figures of life out of the "jelly speck" or vital germ in the womb, or chrysalis of the moth; a kingdom very opposite to that which is conceived of in the speculations of Rationalism, or the dreams of those who are endeavouring to establish a "science of comparative religion." The disciples now began to discover something of the grandeur of self-sacrifice, of the Divine life in the soul of man, of the spiritual work of the Christian calling on earth, of following the Lord in the regeneration of the world. The zeal of consecrating themselves to a life and death of fellowship with their risen Lord in His self-sacrifice, of being His agents and instruments in the establishment of His kingdom, of being partakers with Him in His reign of righteousness, love, and grace, began to glow in their hearts and to rule in their lives. Their dark, dreary gaze into the blank future of blackness was turned into the joy of beholding rising up before them the brightest, most glorious, and blessed future that their hearts could covet or imagination conceive. They now saw as they never anticipated they would see. They saw that the fond dreams they had loved to dream of political place, power, and greatness, were but the conceptions of childhood, nay, the very bubbles of earth, compared with the visions which were now clearly in their view. They had now displayed before them in ever-brightening visions the most illustrious, absorbing, elevating career the finite could pursue or the Infinite could unfold to created eye. They now felt that their intercourse with Christ was to be very different from what it had been before His death. Previously they had been prejudiced and selfish, now they were self-sacrificing and enlightened, ready for any amount of toil and suffering; all their desire being to become like Christ, and to serve Him.

And as with the "eleven," so with the Church in all times and sections: it is not enough for the Church to possess even the mind of Christ; if she is to do His work, she must be pervaded by His Spirit; and so Christ must train her as He did His disciples. The merciful purpose of Heaven to the universe of intelligence was not to be frustrated; the past three years' labours were not to be lost. Christ opened their minds as they were able to bear. He had to breathe upon them, and say, "Receive ye the Holy Ghost." They had to learn that truth can be received only in the love of it, that the spirit of truth must precede the knowledge of truth; ere men can realize a truth, they must inbreathe its spirit. The non-perception of this truth has been the mistake of centuries. Without the spirit of a truth men may study it, and learn much about it, but they can never come to the realization of it. It is only through the truth in the One Spirit that men can have access to the Father.

The mystery of creation is the opening of finite capacity, and the mystery of Christianity is the opening of perverted capacity to the reception of the conditionings of the Infinite. The limitations of the Absolute are not in Himself, but in His entering into and dwelling in the finite or conditioned. And thus the Great Teacher had and has to put up with in the condescension of His instructions, "be it far from the Lord;" and thus Christ had to appear to His disciples, not once, but frequently, not on one, but during "forty days," to qualify them for the descent of the Spirit. The training of the disciples and the Church into the perception of the glorious character, the important work, and deep necessity of self-sacrifice was and is the one work of the Divine Revealer. The difficulties of this work are not in the Divine, but in the carnal. It is in this work that God finds scope for the fuller revelations of Himself. In the manifestations of Himself the Absolute must come under the conditions of revelation, disclose Himself in a series of outcomings, descend into the conflict of the fulness of the times, realize the "hidings" of cloudless Light, experience the anguish of self-sacrifice. And finite capacity to see the Invisible must ascend into the realization of the heights of the Divine, assimilate into the consciousness of fellowship with the Self-sacrificer, drink in the one Spirit, believe on the Son of God; and in this there is illimitable capacity of being filled with "boundless fulness;" the Absolute coming under conditions that the finite may rise out of the limitation of the carnal, into all the "fulness of God" in the infinite and eternal fellowship of the Divine.

What a stretch was there in the conscious descent of the Unconditioned through creation and incarnation to the exclamation of "My God, My God, why hast Thou forsaken Me?" And what possible realization is there, from the faintest consciousness of the quickening with the Divine, to the omniscience of all knowledge? This was realized in the experience of the Incarnate One, in His becoming obedient, complying with the necessary conditions of manifesting the inner depths of the Infinite Essence, or the self-sacrificing of the Godhead, by the things which He suffered. What was known in the experience of the Incarnate One may be learned and realized in the consciousness of the believer in Him. To qualify the "eleven" for the consciousness of glory and bliss in the fellowship with Him of self-sacrifice, and the Church through them, was the object of Christ's returning to them, ascending from them, and sending down the Spirit upon them. It is only as men drink in the Spirit, become one in spirit with Christ, that they can know Him, work His work, enter into the fellowship of His reign. And in this fellowship what glorious occupation, what endless realization, what infinite expanse is there in thus learning Christ!

The effect produced on the apostles by the resurrection and intercourse of Christ is incapable of explanation, except on the admission that "He rose from the dead." If we look at their ignorance of Him and of His work, the tenacity with which they clung to their notion of a political Messiah, of an earthly kingdom, and of a physical reign; if we look at the panic which seized them on the occasion of His arrest, the bewilderment and cowardice they displayed, the amazement they manifested at the intelligence of His resurrection; and if we look at the determination, fortitude, perseverance, self-sacrifice, subsequently exhibited by them in the entire consecration of themselves to His cause, we shall see an effect which could have been produced by no other cause than the fact of His resurrection and "forty days'" intercourse, and the descent of the Holy Ghost.

If it required so much gentleness, skill, and patience in Christ to guide the eleven from their Jewish politico-ecclesiastical notions of the Messianic reign, to self-sacrificing devotion to universal well-being, need we wonder that the Church, instead of passing by a straight and rapid course from pentecost to millennial glory, has had to advance through Gnostic heresy, imperial persecution, patristic struggle, the ambition of ecclesiastical rivalry and jealousy, fed by State connection, the monkish superstitions of Asceticism, and the fearful abuses that arose out of papal arrogance; Romish persecutions, the speculations of the schoolmen, the frightful irregularities of the dark ages, the dreadful bondage of the Inquisition, the abstractions of creedism, the doctrinal controversies, the divisions and sects of the Reformation, the imperfections of modern missions, and whatever else awaits her ere she arrives at her final triumph? The cause of this delay is not in Christ, or in His truth, but in the prejudices of fallen humanity. Man for his recovery needs more than a revelation.

III.

*MAN'S RESPONSIBILITY IN REGARD
TO DIVINE QUICKENING.*

CHAPTER III.

MAN'S RESPONSIBILITY IN REGARD TO DIVINE QUICKENING.

THERE are external operations and influences acting on man, which lead to internal realization and individual action. This fact is so obvious as to need no proof or illustration. There is revolution in the inner nature of man, as well as among the nations of mankind. Men frequently change in regard to the object, principles, and motives of their living. There is such engrossment with the outer things of life as to lead to the neglect of the inner consciousness. And there are such inner realizations as enable the individual to surmount the enslaving allurements of the outer, nay, neglect the necessary requirements of the useful and comfortable in life. It is the inner that makes the outer of life to man even as regards this, and especially in reference to the life to come.

We have mediate fellowship with God, in the intelligent reading of His works, in the clear discernment of the rich and varied combinations of Nature, not as the spontaneous operations of a self-evolving power, but as the evidence of the power and goodness and wisdom of God, and the permanence and immutability of His law. We have mediate and immediate fellowship with God, in the apprehension and realization of His grace in our regeneration, co-operation, communion, assimilation, purification of spiritual enjoyment, enlargement of capacity, elevation of life, and fulness of vision. And we have immediate fellowship with God through the indwelling of His Spirit in our spirits, in His awakening in us the stirrings of the Divine, in His causing to spring in us sympathy, ideas of affection, desire, will, realization, assimilation, oneness of life with Himself.

Man is a religious being, his whole history and experience prove this. His irreligious life no more weakens the force of this truth, than insanity proves that man was not made for reason, or that sickness shows that he is not framed for health, or that ignorance or error demonstrate that he is not constituted for knowledge and truth. The false conditions are not the normal state of man's life; he cannot rest satisfied in any or all of these conditions, but must, by an impulse of soul, strive to escape from each and all of them. Irreligion and prejudice prove that man is constituted for a true religious life, for these do not and cannot satisfy his deepest cravings. He must, by a necessity of nature, struggle to rise above them.

Man is a conscious being. Consciousness underlies all his realizations, and makes them to him what he experiences them to be. He is conscious of his different states of existence, and that these are at times opposite the one to the other. He feels one state of being to be agreeable, and its opposite to be disagreeable. Indeed, it is the difference of feeling or consciousness that causes him to distinguish between his states of existence. He realizes satisfaction in harmony, and dissatisfaction in discord. It is in consciousness that man lives, suffers, or enjoys.

Man is conscious of different, nay, opposite thoughts, feelings, desires, ends, principles, and motives of life. Man also reflects on what occurs within him. He anticipates the future results of his deeds, and sits in judgment over the past actions of his life; and he approves or disapproves of what he is, does, or intends to do. He is often disturbed about the present, hardly knowing what to make of it; he is likewise at times anxious about the results of the past, and deeply concerned with the future.

Man is occasionally conscious of inner awakenings of better thoughts, desires, and resolutions. A little reflection will enable him to perceive that these awakenings of better thoughts, feeling, desire, and resolution are not produced in him by Satan, the world, or the flesh, but by the Spirit of the living God striving with him, affording him "tastings" of "the good mind of God, of the powers of the world to come, making him a partaker of the Holy Ghost" by darting across the vision of his soul waves of light regarding the things of God. In these awakenings the Spirit affords the subject of them the evidence that not only in the Scriptures is God offering to him the gift of eternal life, but also that in the person of His Spirit He is coming to him to quicken him with the Divine life. The awakened is also conscious of what use he makes of these inner risings in his soul; he knows whether he likes or dislikes them, whether he strives to rid himself of them as dull cares, melancholy thoughts, unwelcome visitants intruding themselves into the chambers of his soul, and by engrossing himself with worldly anxieties, frivolous amusements, intemperate indulgences, false counsels, extirpates them from his spirit; or whether he prizes these awakenings of the Spirit of God, endorses and fosters them in his heart by supplication to God for the gift of His Spirit, by study of Christian truth, by acting in accordance with his convictions of right, and carefully shunning whatever is opposed to these inner awakenings, or calculated in the least to injure them.

Man is neither virtuous nor vicious by the mere suggestion or awakening of good or bad thoughts within him. Satan, in tempting the Saviour, suggested forbidden thoughts to Him. But Christ in no way gave the least countenance or encouragement to such. The Spirit of God, striving with sinners, awakens good thoughts within them; but they often refuse to entertain or encourage these in their hearts. It is in clinging to, encouraging, welcoming the good, that men become virtuous, and it is in clinging to, encouraging, welcoming the bad, that men become vicious.

By the one course of action man resists, grieves, quenches, the Holy Ghost; and if he persists in such a course of conduct, commits the sin which is not forgiven, neither in this world, nor in the world to come. How can this sin be forgiven? If the forgiveness of sin is inseparable from the possession of the Divine life in the soul; and if the sinner, as the Spirit of God rouses within him desires after the Divine life, quenches these beginnings or inner awakenings by his resistance of the Holy Ghost, (inasmuch as he quenches the Spirit's quickenings of the Divine life,) he cannot, while he continues to do so, become possessed of the Divine life in his soul, and thus realize the forgiveness of sin. The thing in the very nature of things is an impossibility.

If, on the other hand, by working out what the Spirit of God works in him, to will and to do of God's good pleasure, the sinner endorses, cherishes, fosters, and feeds these awakenings of the Divine life in his soul, he becomes conscious of the Spirit itself "bearing witness with his spirit that he is a child of God," and thus realizes the forgiveness of sin. In his consciousness of the Divine life he has the witness in himself, and knows that he is born of God, has become a new creature, and thus his evidence of regeneration is immediate—the most reliable evidence possible to him.

By perseverance in working out what God by His Spirit works in him, the believer in Christ advances and matures the Divine life in his soul. As the child inhaling a pure atmosphere, feeding on a wholesome and nutritious diet, grows up to manhood, so the believer in Jesus, by co-operating with the Spirit of God, deepens his conscious realizations of the Divine life, and grows into the perfect stature of the fulness of Christ. And in all this he acts in strict accordance with spiritual principles, powers, and laws.

In producing and maturing the Divine life in the soul of the believer, God acts in accordance with the analogies of nature and providence. In these analogies He warns the sinner against trifling with the quickening of the Holy Ghost. There is in the providence of God a great waste, a vast destruction of the embryo or germ of life ever taking place in the natural, to warn man of the possibility of it occurring in the spiritual. In all the grain which is not sown as seed, but consumed for the different purposes of life, in all the spawn of fish and eggs of fowl which are not brought to life, in all the embryo and young of man and beast that fail to come to birth, or are neglected in coming into life, there is a great destruction of the beginning of vitality. The infancy of life, in order to reach maturity, must be gently treated and carefully nurtured. If the seed be not properly sown, it will not germinate into vegetable life, and reach the maturity of the plant. If the new-born child be neglected, it will die. And so, if the quickenings of the Holy Ghost be despised, resisted, and quenched, the germ of the Divine life produced in the soul will never come to maturity, but perish by the suicidal act of the sin against the Holy Ghost.

Those who dislike the awakenings of the spiritual, and quench the beginnings of the Divine life in the soul, may not be aware that they are opposing themselves to God, in the accomplishment of His loftiest and most gracious undertaking, but they are nevertheless doing it; and by so doing they must come short of the realization of the Divine life in its purest, sweetest, most thrilling enjoyment, and thus prepare themselves for the most awful endurance of conscious existence, the ever and anon consciousness of disordered and restless realization of life.

Those who endorse and cultivate the risings of the Divine life in the soul, realize the growth of the highest, most glorious and blessed of all lives, they co-operate with the highest agencies of being, the greatest powers and instrumentalities of nature and of grace, with God, truth, and all holy intelligences. They ever deepen their consciousness of the Divine life in feeding on the Manna of heaven, the Bread of immortal life; and drink of the everlasting streams which flow from the fount of God. They are ever nearing God in their assimilation into His image; they live with God as they ascend into the highest order of conscious existence, as they grow in meetness for the manifestation of the sons of God. They ever become like God in seeing Him as He is, in realizing the Divine, in reigning with Christ over all evil throughout the everlasting ages.

The only principle and true power of the Christian calling is "to work out what God works in us to will and to do;" it is this that enables us to advance in the Divine life, and it is the failing to do this that retards our progress in that life. The work of grace in the believer, the Church, and the world, is the work of God in its design, commencement, continuance, and consummation, and in this work man is the active subject and fellow-worker with God. The Spirit comes to him with the things that are Christ's, to awaken in him the risings of the Divine; and if he endorses and works out what the Spirit of God works in him "to will and to do," he realizes faith in Jesus; but if he rejects or refuses to work out what the Spirit works in him, the Spirit makes no further progress in working in him. The Spirit may continue to work *on* him in producing the risings of the Divine in his soul, but he will not advance one step till he works out "what" the Spirit has awakened in him, and "as" the Spirit requires of him, in working in him to will and to do of God's good pleasure.

And thus it is that the entire work of the believer's assimilation into the Divine image is accomplished by the Spirit of God: in its every degree it is thus produced in the believer's realization of the Divine, in his putting on the Lord Jesus, in his shining in the beauty of holiness, in his letting the light that is in him shine around him so as to allure others to Jesus. He is, in his consciousness of the Divine, wholly the workmanship of the Spirit of God. If he work out as and only as the Spirit works in him, then will he make rapid progress in the Divine life, and be greatly honoured to glorify God in his day and generation: but if from yielding to other influences he halts in working out, or endeavours to work out after his own conceptions or the opinions of man, then will the Spirit cease His workings in him, until God, by His providential dealings, leads him to repent of his wickedness, and brings him to work out as the Spirit works in him to will and to do. This view of God's dealings with His children enables us to see the consistency of God, in what otherwise would appear strange in His training of His children, and providence over His church.

These awakenings of the Spirit of God originate in the soul of man the beginnings of the grandest, most Godlike work of the Godhead; no achievement of time or eternity can for one moment be compared with the work of God,—with these awakenings of the Spirit of God in the soul of man, with the quickenings of the human spirit through the risings of the Divine life. This work of the Spirit effects the reconciliation of the spirit of man with the Spirit of God; secures the harmony of the life of man with the outgoings of God, with the principles, laws, and ends of being and doing. It enables the believer to do the will of God, in working out what God works in him to will and to do of God's good pleasure, to take his part in, and accomplish his portion of, that work which displays the supreme majesty, glory, and delight of the Godhead, which enables man to choose, will, and enjoy with God, as he co-operates with Him in the most wondrous, sublime, and glorious of all the undertakings possible to God or man.

Is there anything within the wide range of possible existence, that can be of such importance to man as the endorsing and working out these suggestions, which the Spirit of God awakes in his inmost consciousness, to enable him to begin and work out his own salvation, and to aid in the deifying his own and the life of others? What is there in time, that is worth one moment's preference to the life of God in the soul of man? And this working out what the Spirit of God works in him to will and to do, is absolutely necessary to the believer's realizing the Divine life. To enjoy the beautiful, the euphonic, the artistic, the sublime, we must have and cultivate the taste for such; to enjoy the heroic, the grand, the self-sacrificing, in moral conduct, we must have the love for and consciousness of such deeds. And it is only while we are members of the Church below, while we are in this world of sin, that we possess the opportunities of co-operating with Christ in the sublime of self-sacrifice, and of enjoying fellowship with the Godhead in the most glorious possible achievements of God. It must be kept in mind that in order to His performance of His portion of this work, the Brightness of the Father's glory had to come into this world of sin and suffering, and yield Himself up in self-sacrifice to the will of His foes. It was not in heaven, nor in the indolence of repose on earth, but in the sphere of self-sacrifice, that the well-beloved Son of God yielded Himself to the injustice of sinners, that He might draw them to God, and by so doing achieve His wondrous work, win His glory, and realize His bliss. And it is only while men are in this world, that they can imitate the Incarnate One in the grandeur of His self-sacrifice.

And in this view of God's dealing with man by His Spirit we are enabled to see the true nature of human responsibility. Man cannot immediately create power, alter the conditions of his life, nor place himself in relations different from what he finds himself to be in; but he can resist or yield to, and co-operate with, the powers bearing on him, and thus avail himself of his circumstances, and by so doing, better or deteriorate his condition. He cannot command the Spirit's influence, but he can resist or yield to truth or error. He knows whether he allows the light that darts across his mind to guide his life, or refuses to give it a place among his thoughts. He can choose between dispositions, ideas, motives, principles, and actions, and he must realize in accordance with his choice. He can form a combination, but he cannot control or alter the operations of the powers acting in combination. He must realize the benefit of yielding to right power, or the bane of giving himself up to evil influence, and his conscience will tell him that he merits these results.

If there had been no carnality, there would have been no need of quickening. And if renewing had not been in overcoming and expelling carnality from the immortal spirit, there would have been no scope for the display of Divine grace, wisdom, and long-suffering on the one hand, or for selfishness, ascetic abuse, and perversion on the other. Humanity in its fall and recovery is the "area" where the grandest achievements of God and man are wrought out, and in which the fullest operations of responsibility are realized.

Man's obligation and responsibility in regard to the Spirit of God are cautiously to avoid every practice that has a tendency to increase his aversion and opposition to the Spirit. As the Spirit of God is the Spirit of love, light, liberty, purity, generosity, he is to avoid the giving way to enmity, the cherishing of prejudice, inordinate affections or dispositions, intemperance, narrow-mindedness, miserliness, *i.e.*, selfishness; he is to cultivate whatever has a tendency to open up his heart, his mind, his life, to the reception of the Spirit of God. And man knows well that he can either do or refuse to do such things. Every human being is conscious of a power to yield to or resist external influence; he knows that his life and character are in accordance with his reception or refusal of influence, of idea, of example, and in this he feels that his responsibility rests.

IV.

THE DIVINE RE-POSSESSING ITSELF OF THE HUMAN.

CHAPTER IV.

*THE DIVINE RE-POSSESSING ITSELF OF THE HUMAN.**

WE are familiar with indwelling. We have numerous examples of its different phases. An individual enters into and dwells in a house. Light, when the shutters are opened, comes into and dwells in a room. Electricity enters and runs along the iron rod. Heat penetrates and pervades many things. Truth enters into and dwells in the mind of man. Love comes into the heart, and life into the consciousness or conscious capacity of humanity. But they do not all enter into and take up their abode after the same fashion.

There are numerous manifestations of superior to inferior existence. It is as the higher enters into the inferior life, and assimilates it to itself, that it raises it in the scale of being. And there is the discernment and appropriation of such manifestations; so also there is near, sweet, full communion of life with life, by means of the

* See "Science of Spiritual Life," chap. xviii.

appropriation of manifestation, and assimilation of life with life through appropriation. It is only as the inferior life assimilates to the superior, that it can hold satisfying fellowship with the superior life entering into and dwelling in it.

God manifests Himself in His works of creation, in His providence over the nations, in His Son, and by His Spirit; He manifests Himself externally and internally to man. His external are subservient to His internal manifestations. In His external manifestations He conditions Himself under certain limitations, comes under different forms of finite existence. The Absolute or Infinite has no forms, but the finite necessarily has: it cannot exist but in forms; wherever it appears, it appears in the limitation of forms. Forms are necessary to the manifestations of God, at least to His external manifestations. When one mind manifests itself to another, it must necessarily condition itself in certain forms, or come under the limitations of thought expressed in language, written or spoken, in order to enter into and dwell in other minds. In like manner God the Infinite, in order to manifest the perfection of His Being, must come under the limitations of the finite. Only thus does He become recognizable by it.

The connection of matter with mind is mysterious, and to us unknown. If mind for its manifestations be dependent on matter, it is in no way under the control of matter. Mind moves matter as it wills. Matter is not self-active, but inert. Mind is essentially active. The thoughts of one mind pass into forms of sound or written words, to enter into the apprehension of other minds. In thinking, the subjective of mind becomes its objective. And in the process of one mind expressing itself to another, it embodies its objective so as to become the objective of other minds. And the believing mind apprehending its received objective, becomes in its subjective one with the revealing mind. Matter is thus the medium of mind communicating with mind.

God manifests the gracious purpose of His heart, and the enmity of sin, by means of self-sacrifice. We cannot conceive of God adopting another or a more efficacious method of displaying the gracious purpose of His heart, or the bitter enmity of sin, than He has done in the self-sacrifice of His Son. And thus it was that His well-beloved Son was delivered up to the power of the carnal mind, by the determinate counsel and foreknowledge of God. God manifests the long-suffering of His gracious purpose concerning the salvation of man in and by the persistent striving of His Spirit.

The Son in His incarnate being, sayings, and doings, manifests the being, purpose, and will of the Father. He who sees the Son sees the Father, he who hears the Son hears the Father, and he who receives the Son receives the Father also. The Spirit, by working that faith in man which appropriates the Son, manifests to the inner consciousness of the believer the highest perfections of the Godhead. In His inner workings the Spirit enables the believer in Jesus to appropriate the lineaments and properties of the Divine, as He awakes in his consciousness the realizations of immediate fellowship with the Divine, and develops the life of God in his soul.

The Spirit wakens in the soul of the believer the beginnings of the Divine life, by producing in him the risings of sympathy, of disposition, of affection, of thought, of feeling, of desire, of aspiration, of purpose, of resolution, the will, of becoming one in conscious life with God.

The Spirit, by inducing the believer to endorse, foster, and develop the Divine awakenings in his soul, works in him to will and to do in accordance with God's good pleasure; and thus establishes the believer in the deepening consciousness and bliss of the life of God in his soul. In thus working, the Spirit produces in the inner being of the believer, the ear, the eye, the palate, the intellect, the soul—in one word, the consciousness through which the Divine life is realized. The Spirit thus re-creates the believer in Jesus in the image of God, or creates him anew in that through which God comes into the believer in His Son, and manifests Himself to him; and that through which the believer in Christ ascends to the vision of God; that by which the believer and God become one in the consciousness of the Divine life.

The work of the Spirit in the believer in Jesus is the highest possible doing of the Godhead in the manifestation of the Divine. These awakenings in the believer in God's Son are the lineaments, elements, properties, and functions of the Divine life; to manifest which to the inner life of man the brightness or subjective had to become the objective of the Father's glory, had to descend to the cross; and to impart which to the inmost consciousness of the believer, the Spirit had to strive persistently, and suffer grief, in order to make the objective of the Divine the subjective of the human.

The importance of these inner awakenings may in some measure be discerned in reason, without being realized in life; but the discernment of the importance of these in reason is far inferior to the realization of them in life.

In imparting these lineaments to the believer in Jesus, the Spirit quickens his life with the very properties and functions of the life of God. In the consciousness of which the life of the believer becomes one in consciousness with the conscious life of God. And thus the believer in God's Son enters into a oneness of spirit, mind, and life with God, realizes the beginnings of the perfection of the Divine life in his soul, the foretaste of the glory which is yet to be revealed.

To the production of these elements of the Divine life in the soul of man, Creation, Providence, Revelation, Atonement, Ascension of the Son, and descent of the Spirit of God, have all been subordinate and subservient. How unspeakable then is their importance! The highest attainments in material being, in the sentient, social, national life of man, in the world of mind, in the angelic ranks, are as nothing in comparison with these re-created lineaments of the Divine in the soul of the believer. In the consciousness of these man enters into the nearest possible likeness to God. He ascends to the loftiest pinnacle in the temple of being and life, rises far above all other finite existence in the grandeur and greatness of his soul.

In the mouldings of matter the substance is plastic, but in the creation and education of life, the substance is co-operative, especially in the highest of all creation and life. Greece could see and appreciate the glory of the physical figure of man, she had even dim glimpses of the surpassing grandeur of his intellectual genius and greatness, but she had not the most distant glimpse of the high altitude of his conscious fellowship with God in His manifestations through faith, and in realization of the most wondrous displays of the Divine.

The conscious realization in the inner and manifestation in the outer life of the believer of these properties and perfections of the Divine in his soul, is the enjoyment of the nearest fellowship, of the purest bliss of the finite with the Infinite, of the human with the Divine. There is no possession possible to man, which either for its own importance or that of its results, can be compared for one moment with the possession of these inner awakenings of the indwelling of the Spirit of God in the spirit of man.

And there is no Divine life in man, no religious

action performed by him, that is acceptable to God, or profitable to himself, but what is the manifestion of the Spirit's awakening in his soul. The consciousness of this inner life, and of its outer manifestations, is the realization of salvation, the enjoyment of the saints in light, the only appearance with Christ in the glory of His reign. The consciousness of this inner realization and outer manifestation is the entrance of the believer into the perfections of the Divine, the beginning of being for ever with the Lord.

If the fall of man was not necessary, it was at least subservient to the highest manifestations of the Divine, the most striking display of the self-sacrificing of the Godhead, to the creation in the human of the most receptive capacity for the realizations of the nearest, fullest, and most blissful indwelling of the Divine.

The entrance on a lofty condition of spiritual existence, through strife and conflict, by self-denial and self-sacrifice, is a far nobler and much more efficient preparation for its realization and enjoyment, than the being thrown into it by the mere accident of birth, without any individual effort to secure it on the part of him who enters upon it. This is the underlying principle for the permission of persecution, the sustaining power of the lofty heroism of the martyr, and of the sympathy which is felt for the sufferer, as well as of the admiration in which his conduct is universally held. And yet Christian society, with all its means of information, has much to learn regarding this phase of Divine Providence.

Communion with God, in the realization of His self-sacrificing, redemptive love, is possible to the believer only in this sinful world. The existence of evil is to the discipline of the believer, in his progress to the perfection of the Christian life, what atmosphere is to the flight of the bird. It is only in overcoming evil that we can realize the victory of faith. Hence it is through tribulation that the believer enters the kingdom.

God works in the material, in endless variety, and in doing so produces numerous lovely and magnificent results; the most stupendous of which is what the Psalmist speaks of when he says, " I am fearfully and wonderfully made. My substance was not hid from Thee, when I was made in secret, and curiously wrought in the lowest parts of the earth. Thine eyes did see my substance, yet being unperfect; and in Thy book all my members were written, which in continuance were fashioned, when as yet there was none of them." Yet none of the grandeur of this work is seen or known in consciousness when it is being "curiously wrought." And so of the far more grand and illustrious work which is being wrought out in the training of the sons of God for their manifestation in glory. This glorious work of transformation in the re-creation of the sons of God is scorned by the world, and far from being clearly discerned and understood by the Church, but it is none the less wondrous in its nature, Divine in its character, and glorious in its consummation. This work is advancing in the silent majesty of its unobserved grandeur, unknown or little regarded now, but will be seen in its full-orbed splendour when brought conspicuously before the gaze of the assembled universe.

To perceive the vast importance of the present condition of Christian living and working, the believer and the Church require to rise to a clearer vision of the profound principles and deepening realizations of the Divine in Christ Jesus. And to acquire such they must cease to resist, and more vigorously co-operate with, the Spirit of God in His striving to raise the Church into fuller realizations of the spiritual and Divine. They must drink deeper into the Spirit, realize more fervent communion with the Spirit, and manifest more of the life of the Spirit.

All love of worldly vain show, all desire to conform to its selfish customs, all striving after its power, distinctions, honours, and rewards, in preference to the inner attainments of the Divine, and manifestations of the grace of self-sacrifice, is a resistance of the Spirit, whether it be in the formal of religious life, the emulations of ecclesiastical aims, or the contentions about the doctrines of Christianity. It is only in yielding up to the higher quickening of the Divine that Christian society can rise to the enjoyment of nearer, fuller, and sweeter fellowship with God in the purest, loftiest, and divinest of His being, doing, and realizing, whether in this or the life to come. Life can be realized only in and by conformity with the conditions of its progress. In the consciousness of life in communion with God we have the inmost of the spiritual, the clearest visions of the realized indwellings of the Father, Son, and Spirit. We have the conscious realization of the Father, Son, and Spirit coming into us, and making their abode with us, in the manifestations of their indwelling presence.

Desire for an end manifests itself in the employment of the necessary means. It goes out through will, manifests itself in volition, producing means for the accomplishment of its end. In this way God reproduced Himself in man, creating him in His own likeness. He thus wrought His way at first to His indwelling in the human, producing the universe with man at its head.

God was expelled from His indwelling in the human by man's transgression of the law of fellowship. By desiring something different from a condition of fellowship, the individual so desiring begins to move out of that fellowship, and thus passes from its realization into another condition ere he is aware of what is going on within him. In this way man prepared himself for the deed by which he passed from a condition of agreeable fellowship with God, into one of disagreeable fellowship with himself, with God, and all that stands in the way of his selfishness.

God wrought His way to His re-indwelling in the human by a more immediate outgoing of Himself in incarnation. The essential instead of the mere vital of the Divine took up His abode in the immaculate child, and thus the essentially Divine developed the human in undeviating conformity with Himself, and in this He displayed what the human in perfect accord with the Divine could be, do, and realize.

This incarnation of the Divine in the human was all that the Father's heart desired. He rested with fullest complacency in the life of His Son, and He exulted in the self-sacrificing death of Calvary, because it was the fullest possible manifestation of His gracious love. This exultation, however, was not in the suffering but in the heroism of that death.

The objective Divine becomes the objective human through man's believing in the Son of God. Faith in Jesus realizes the invisible of the Divine in the consciousness of the believing human. The object of faith becomes subject to the believer in his conscious oneness of realization with God in his soul, and thus the subjective human becomes one with the subjective of God. The believer in God's Son thus lives the life of God. Through God's loving him and his loving God, God dwells in him and he in God. Between God and the believer in Christ there is a oneness of conscious life realized in a similarity of mind and identity of heart. The conscious life of the *adopted* is the reflection of the conscious life of the *only begotten* Son of the Father. The Father and the Son having taken up their abode with the believer, in and through means of his reconciliation with them, they are one in their enjoyment of conscious life, or in the fellowship of the self-sacrificing of the Divine.

V.

THE TRUE AND THE FALSE OF AMBITION.

CHAPTER V.

THE TRUE AND THE FALSE OF AMBITION.

MAN, by the deepest instincts of his nature, and the highest ends of his existence, is an ambitious being; but he knows not how to pursue the true object of his ambition, nor to gratify aright the ruling passion of his heart. He does not perceive that there is a far more illustrious way of displaying ambition than in vieing with one another in vainglory about human attainments and earthly possessions. Man requires to have a proper object of ambition made known to him, and the best method of pursuing the high end of his existence. In this lies the profound truth and important principle of his well-being.

Man has to struggle, and to struggle severely, with or against evil. Man cannot use evil to his advantage. This in the nature of things is an impossibility. He may make it the occasion, but never the instrument, of good. And this he can do only in connection with self-sacrifice. Self-sacrifice is the only deed that enables man to take occasion from evil to realize the highest possible good, and live the noblest of all conceivable lives. He thus can give full scope to his ambition, and rise to the loftiest condition of existence in the pursuit of his chief good.

Selfishness animating the sordid spirit of man has produced the most hideous forms of crime, debauchery, and baseness, that have marred the life of man on earth, and darkened with the foulest blots the pages of human history and biography. Selfishness can only lead to failure, disappointment, and ruin; ambition moved by selfishness has led to illustrious achievements, the display of gigantic powers, and the acquisition of dazzling fame, but only by severe effort, at great expense, terminating in disappointment and sadness. In the lofty aims and alluring enterprises which captivate the spirit of man in the various departments of life, both in Church and State, he has performed deeds which have attracted the gaze and drawn forth the admiration of multitudes of observers. But man in the performance of the most illustrious deeds of selfish ambition has ever failed to secure lasting benefits to his race, or permanent honour to himself. From the arena of the most startling exploits of selfish ambition he has had to retire under darkening clouds of discomfiture, in the chagrin of conscious failure. And whenever the motives and principles of his deeds of selfish ambition have come to light, they have awakened the strongest feelings of condemnation, if not of scorn and contempt.

The deeds of selfish ambition, from the initial act of covetousness and sin of our first parents down to the present moment, have only been fraught with evil. The Nimrods of Babel Tower, the Pharaohs of Egypt, the Nebuchadnezzars of Babylon, the Dariuses of Persia, the Alexanders of Greece, the Cæsars of Rome, the bishops, cardinals, and popes of Italy, etc., have all through selfish ambition fearfully perverted their powers and opportunities, brought ruin on themselves, and injury on others. If proof were necessary, we have only to refer to Cardinal Wolsey's exclamation, "If I had served my God with half the zeal I have served my king, He wouldn't have abandoned me;" also the recorded confession of Æneas Sylvius Piccolomini, "While I was a priest I had some good hopes of salvation; when I became a cardinal, I began to doubt it; but since I became pope I have no hope at all;" or to Napoleon's reflections in St. Helena on the principles of empire.

On the other hand, ambition animated by the spirit of self-sacrifice has produced the noblest, the most sublime, heroic, and happy characters of time; characters which have won the highest honours, secured the most lasting benefits for the human race, and drawn forth the spontaneous admiration and gratitude of all after-ages and generations. The self-sacrificing spirit of the missionary of the Cross ennobles his life and benefits the scene of his self-sacrificing labours. The influence of such spirits as those of Livingstone, Duff, Paterson, Williams, Schwartz, and Xavier are felt, and will for ages to come exert the most telling influence on mankind for good. The self-sacrificing spirit of Christian philanthropists, as in the case of John Howard, has and will continue to shed a benign influence on all susceptible society, and bring untold blessings on innumerable multitudes of unborn humanity. The self-sacrificing spirit of Christian reformers, as that of Luther, has burst asunder the bonds of the most galling bondage, emancipated millions from degrading superstition, and exhibited a devotion and courage to the highest interests of God and man, which has commanded and will continue to command the homage of admiring myriads. The courage which could declare its resolution to proceed to Worms in the face of innumerable frowning fiends, and display singly and alone that undaunted magnanimity which awed that august assembly, irresistibly compels admiration and applause. The self-sacrificing spirit of the martyrs of Christ, from that of Stephen, calling upon Jesus to forgive his murderers, to that of Cranmer, who in a lofty indignation at his momentary weakness of recantation, burned off the hand that signed the record of his frailty, has led to the performance of the most heroic deeds, and set the most illustrious examples that earth can ever witness. No tongue can tell or pen describe the innumerable blessings which the self-sacrificing spirit of the martyrs of Jesus Christ has conferred on mankind. The deeds of heroic grandeur, the benefits of lasting worth, the example, which the self-sacrificing spirit of the Apostle of the Gentiles has bestowed on the human race, will require eternity itself to disclose; and all the benefits which philanthropy, literature, art, science, and philosophy have conferred on the race, have been bestowed through self-denial and self-sacrifice.

And when even in thought we call before us, and dwell in meditation upon, the self-sacrificing spirit of the Son of man, we are constrained to prostrate ourselves in the deepest adoration, admiration, love, and gratitude. In His felt presence we are fired with His spirit, allured by His example, dignified and blessed in the conscious imitation of His life. As in the contemplation of His illustrious character and the grandeur of His work we are constrained to enquire, how is it that He alone of all that ever appeared on earth, understood the true use of ambition, and how it was that He turned it to its proper account? To such an enquiry there is but one reply: "For the joy that was set before Him, He endured the cross, despising the shame."

The great want of this age of self-seeking enquiry is the proper understanding of the true sphere, right action, and proper results of self-sacrificing ambition. Christian life in its consecrated devotion meets the want, and affords to the human spirit all that is necessary to a noble career in the formation of an illustrious character, a blissful consciousness in the boundless expanse of the soul. The spirit of Christian devotedness has only to consecrate itself in enlightened self-sacrificing zeal to the glory of God in the bliss of man, in order to perform Divine deeds, both in the humblest and in the highest walks of life, and in so doing to realize the purest fellowship with the infinite and eternal God in the attainment of the loftiest destiny of being and life.

Christ alone knew how to take occasion from evil to turn ambition to its proper account. He saw that notwithstanding the hateful character of evil, it may be made the occasion of the very highest possible good; and that this world of sinful life, if not the only, is the fairest region in all God's universe for taking occasion from evil to achieve the highest good. He saw that the virtues of patience, of forbearance, of forgiveness, etc., could never have been cultivated and matured if evil had never existed. He was well aware that the achievement of the noblest deeds, the formation of the loveliest character, the breaking open of the fountain of the purest bliss, the alluring of men from the selfishness of the Satanic to the self-sacrificing of the Divine, could never have been, if there had been no evil to contend with.

The noblest attributes of Godhead would not have been known out of the consciousness of God Himself, the operations of Divine love in the fullest manifestations of itself could not have been disclosed, the sublime conception of grace reigning through righteousness would not have been realized, the transformation of the rebel into the filial child could not have been accomplished, the most glorious achievement of Godhead, in the perfection and blessedness of sinful human souls, could not have been known, had evil not existed.

These glorious ends could only have been achieved by the spirit of self-sacrifice animating the soul of ambition. The graces of patience, forbearance, fortitude, forgiveness, love of enemies, blessing them that curse, praying for them that despitefully use and evil entreat, are possible only through self-sacrifice, and self-sacrifice in its most perfect form is possible only through the existence and operations of evil. But for the cherishing and manifesting the spirit of self-sacrifice in the meek and patient endurance of evil, Christ Himself could never have lived His true life, formed His sublime character, risen to the superhuman height of exclaiming, "Father, forgive them, for they know not what they do."

The false conceptions and teachings of not a few of Christian dogmatists regarding Christian humility, together with the perversions of the principles of sacrifice in the popular theology of the Church, have formed an incubus which has fearfully oppressed and enervated the energies of Christendom, and threatened the extinction of the very life of the Church itself.

Love seeks, if it does not demand, nay, necessitate, the occasion of self-sacrifice. Love never attains its true altitude, never expresses its true self, never realizes its purest satisfaction, never knows itself, till it suffers on behalf of its objects. Self-sacrifice is the deed in which love outbreathes its true self. This is true of human as well as of Divine love. The lover, in the measure of his true affection, is ever ready to sacrifice himself for or on behalf of the object of his heart. This is the true explanation of the incarnate life, death, and ascension of God's own Son, the voluntary self-sacrifice of the Godhead. Without this sacrifice, as far as we can see, God would never have outwardly realized the inmost depths of His own Being, crowned His workings with a display worthy of His love, *i.e.*, Himself. In this, however, He is not self-seeking. This is impossible to love, which in its very essence is self-devotion. There are mysteries in love which are yet to be learned.

May this fact not throw some light on the true solution of the permission of evil? It was not from love of it, nor indifference to evil, that it was permitted to invade God's fair universe. It was allowed an existence, that occasion might be taken from its presence to work out the highest, sublimest, divinest ends of being, that Godhead might realize its inmost being in the fullest expression of itself on behalf of rebel existence.

If so, what a future opens up before us in the hereafter of the Christian Church! When the sublime importance of the principle of self-sacrifice shall be understood, and felt pervading and influencing the ranks of all Christian Society, then Rationalism, Formalism, Creedism, Ecclesiasticism, Moralism, Asceticism, Pietism, will fall into and occupy their inferior places. The spirit of vainglory, rivalry, strife and contention among brethren will become unknown, immorality in conduct, trickery in trade, undue advantage in commerce, crime in social life, selfish deeds among Christians, will be seen in their true unworthiness, and so frowned upon as to be banished out of the Church. Intelligence will be cultivated, brotherly love will prevail, so that communion in a refined, exalted, and just character, will be all but universally rejoiced in. For while Christians will still have to bear their cross in crucifying the flesh, with its affections and lusts, they will joy and rejoice in self-sacrifice with joy unspeakable and full of glory. As the great Self-sacrificer, under the pressure of His outer sufferings, realized the more fully the deep and abundant welling up of the inner streams of bliss, so will the joy of His disciples living in the nearer imitation of Him abound in them the more.

When once the spirit of self-sacrifice as the true principle of Christian life in a sinful world is properly understood, a new atmosphere will be created in the Church, and a new influence breathed by the heart of the brotherhood. To the extent in which this influence shall be felt and acted on, hypocrisy, meanness, and fraud will be found impossible. There will then be no need of gilding the Christian life, or of getting up in the Church attractions to draw to or retain within her pale the youth of her communities, nor will there be any need of devising institutions or framing laws to regulate the intercourse of brethren. Intelligence, piety, brotherly kindness, godliness, will be so pure, exalted, and appreciated, that the power of self-sacrifice being all but universally felt, acknowledged, and delighted in, the Church, as in the beginning, will attract mankind within her pale by myriads.

The principle of self-sacrifice will then take occasion, from existing evil, to display its true character, and accomplish its Divine work so as to command the homage of all. It will in this crucifixion of self encounter and subdue the evils in the life of the individual, the Church, and the world, so as to bring the Christian communities into resemblance with the apostolic times. It was the spirit of self-sacrifice reigning in the Church of those days, that strengthened and glorified her in the sight of men. The ambition of aiding in effecting such Godlike results, of acquiring such glory, and of diffusing such bliss, will baptize men with the spirit of self-sacrifice to such a degree as will enable them to see that it was the spirit of this lofty ambition that, animating the Son of man in His wondrous life and amazing death, exalted Him in the view of the universe, and made Him the recognized principle and acknowledged power of all that is dignified and illustrious in the true life of man.

This world may have been needed for the highest education of the entire universe; the need be of which is not grounded in the Infinite or Absolute, but in the limited, and consequently imperfect, condition of the finite. If the principle of self-sacrifice is to occupy so lofty a position, and effect so glorious a work on earth, will its power be unfelt in other spheres and periods of existence? We cannot imagine that its operations will be limited to this terrestrial ball, or to the brief period of time. If the principle of self-sacrifice be the very essence of love, the inmost virtue of the Godhead itself, the most glorious element of the highest character, the most blessed ingredient of all exalted life, may it not be destined to reign throughout the entire universe of being, and to bind together, not in a dead uniformity, but in the rich diversity and varied degrees of life, all the orders and ranks of spiritual existence; and thus embracing all finite orders of intelligence, extend throughout all time and the whole of eternity?

The imperfections of human frailty subserve the manly struggles of earthly life, in which self-sacrifice finds its true sphere of operation. It certainly is far more noble to struggle through tribulation into the kingdom, in the true discipline of noble powers which qualify for the loftiest conditions of conscious being and life, than to be brought into the enjoyment of conscious innocence of life by mere submission to or plastic compliance with creative power, leading into the calm security of angelic life. Is it not amazing that the theologians of the Christian Church could have so shut their eyes to the grandeur of Christ's earthly life, as to fall into dreams of the vast superiority of angelic experience to Christian life on earth, and thus lead to a mawkish sentimentalism, which has induced the weaker members of Christ to long to be away in heaven, instead of embracing their fair and enviable opportunities of imitating their Lord in winning, through self-sacrifice, the brighter diadems of glory?

We advance a step further than the defence of self-sacrifice from the point of its importance and underlying power of bliss, and assert the absolute necessity of it, not the mere necessity as arising out of the wants and circumstances of fallen humanity, but the necessity which is grounded in the deeper depths of immortal being and life, the inmost nature of the infinite and eternal Godhead. We would shrink from writing presumptuously on so mysterious a theme, but we cannot forego the opportunity of giving expression to the conviction that as philosophy has hitherto underlain the intepretation of the deep mysteries of revelation, the time is not distant when the teaching and principles of philosophy will be received only in as far as they quadrate with the profounder truths of Christianity.

Why is the love of glory so deeply and indestructibly imbedded in the nature of man? why does he in every sphere and circumstance of life long for (and seek after) distinctions? why was creation called into existence in its present peculiar form? man permitted to fall, and suffering to prevail in the world? why did incarnate Deity travail in the greatness of His strength, mighty to save? May it not have been because there is in the Godhead a yearning to display the inmost glory of the Absolute Essence, a longing of Infinite and Eternal Love to realize itself in the consciousness of self-sacrifice, that it might raise its own expressed image into the nearest possible consciousness of its own life, in an everlasting and uninterrupted fellowship with itself, not from self-seeking, which is contrary to the very essence of love, but in the deepest devotion of itself to the supreme glory and bliss of the objects of its purest affection?*

Man cannot satisfy himself with mere existence, with mere painless existence, no, nor with mere sinless life. If he reads aright the deepest instincts of his spirit, he will detect yearnings after the conscious possession of the virtues of heroic martyrdom. To become conscious of such he will readily sacrifice his life, his all. We pen these lines not in ignorance of the bent of popular preaching, which paints heaven to the eager listener as a most desirable state of

* See chap. ix.

indolent repose; but such teaching, while it rivets the attention and captivates the hearts of the thoughtless multitudes, will not meet the deep cravings of man's immortal spirit within, satisfy his indestructible yearnings after distinction, nor raise him to the elevation of the spiritual and Divine.

The enjoyment of innocence, the happiness of blameless existence, is the bliss of angelic being and seraphic life; but man, created in the highest order of finite existence, and formed for fellowship with the Godhead in its purest, deepest, sweetest bliss, for the nearest possible approach of the created to the uncreated life, must crave after a loftier condition of existence and life, than that of mere blameless being or innocent living. His proper sphere of action in the Church below is the martyrdom of self-sacrifice, and in the Church above, to realize the full consciousness of having so lived upon the earth, as to have washed his robes in the blood of the Lamb. It is then he will possess the clear vision of the glorious results of self-sacrifice. The song of the redeemed in heaven is a song which no one can learn but the "hundred and forty and four thousand which were redeemed from the earth." Man is created for fellowship with the Godhead, and this can be enjoyed in its highest bliss only in the consciousness of self-sacrifice.

The true condition of believers on earth is to be blameless and harmless, the sons of God in the midst of a crooked and perverse generation, among whom they are to shine as lights in the world, holding forth the word of life. This is a condition of being and life which is possible to those only who live in the practice of self-sacrifice. This state of being is very different from that of the unfallen intelligences of heaven, in all their glory and bliss. It is the most illustrious phase of life possible to finite or infinite existence in time or in eternity.

Of course such a condition of life can only be, in the very nature of things, temporary self-sacrifice; martyrdom, a suffering life, misconception, and unmerited reproach, are not and cannot be in themselves desirable. They are submitted to only as a means to an illustrious end, yielded to as necessary for the opening up of the deeper springs of consciousness in the soul, and leading to the clearer discernment of the profounder nature of things, the more distant possibilities of existence. Obscurity and suffering can therefore be only temporary, and as such they are offered to believers on earth as the most favourable conditions, while they are in the Church below, of becoming like Christ; inasmuch as these conditions afford the disciple of Jesus the most apt opportunities of imitating his Lord, and becoming identified with Him in His most glorious and blessed consciousness. But who in the professing Church below believes this? and who of those who do believe it, eagerly seize, like Paul, their present opportunities?

This is the doctrine which is needed by the Church, and which meets the wants of the world, which is fitted to enlist the energies of all Christians, in the different spheres of life; which speaks to the deepest instincts of humanity, and which sheds a flood of light on God's dealings with man—nay, opens up to our view the inmost recesses of the very heart of Godhead Itself. Let every believer in Christ realize the power of this doctrine, and the worldliness of the Church is at an end, she will become animated once more with apostolic zeal, and her glorious work will be understood and performed in its true spirit. The attempts to moralize Christian truth, and the preaching of such doctrine for the ascetic life of the Church, will not elevate her in the view of the world, nor equip her for the performance of her true work.

It is no valid objection to such teaching to say that it is inconsistent with the immutability and absolute perfection of the Godhead. Scripture furnishes us with the means of meeting such objections; for while the Bible teaches us clearly the absolute perfection and immutability of the Divine essence, it also shows us that life is a consciousness which, while it can be realized in its infinitude and eternity by the Absolute in Himself, required for its manifestation in fellowship with the finite, the conditionings of an outcome in the developments of time.

The end was known to God, was present with Him, in the beginning; His delights were with the children of men. Christ, in the consciousness of Godhead, is the Lamb slain from the foundation of the world. In the consciousness of the Infinite all was ever present; but in the outcome of the Infinite in the Absolute, conditioning Himself, the Eternal comes into the temporary, that the temporary may pass into the Eternal. And in the elevation of the finite and temporal into the consciousness of life and fellowship with the Infinite and Eternal, there must be the outgoing or conditioning of the Absolute in a creation, incarnation, and manifestation of life, a proclamation, a belief of the faith, or fellowship in self-sacrifice.*

This doctrine shows us that it is only those

* See chap. ix.

who live the life of Christ on earth, that can, in the very nature of things, realize the oneness of consciousness with Him in the glorious and blessed reign in heaven. It shows us the deep necessity for diligence and fidelity in our Christian calling here below; and will secure believers from contentions among themselves, as well as save them from resting in the mere admiration of the martyr, and especially from the danger of making him an idol of worship, which it is to be feared is done by many. On the contrary, it will induce the Church, while admiring the heroism of the martyr, to strive to surpass his devotion, and coveting earnestly the better gifts, labour in fervent zeal to imitate in even higher measure the example of the Great Sacrificer Himself.

VI.

THE CHARACTER OF SELF-SACRIFICE.

CHAPTER VI.

THE CHARACTER OF SELF-SACRIFICE.

SELF in God is not to be confounded with self in the sinful creature. Self in God denotes the perfection of His Being, and self-love in God signifies His love of the perfection of His Being and doing, especially of His self-sacrificing devotion for the good of man. Self-love in the sinful creature denotes the preference of individual likings, methods, and ends, irrespective of, nay, in opposition to, the nature of things, the constituted order of the universe, the law and authority of God. Self in God is noble, and worthy of His Being. Self in man is ignoble and degrading. Self in the sinful creature is an idol, a delusion which has no existence except in his own diseased imagination. Adherence to self leads the sinner to act against reality, the reality of the Infinite and Eternal, of the creaturely and vital against the requirements of law and perfection, against the conditions of pure enjoyment of all existence.

Self in the creature being that which drags its dupes down to the lowest depths of degradation and woe, the sacrifice of self in man must necessarily be elevating both in the measure and manner of its operations. Self-denial and self-sacrifice in the sinner is the giving up of the idols which deceive him and lead him to war with God, the constituted order of the universe, the nature of man, and the principles of universal well-being. Self-sacrifice or denial in the Christian is the giving up of all in him which conflicts with his own and the well-being of others; it also denotes the patient submission to wrong, that the wrong-doer may be reclaimed to God. Self-sacrifice thus implies no indifference to the perfection or comfort of life, but only the parting with those habits of fallen humanity which interfere with man's true standing, enjoyment, and influence for good, in a correct and beneficent life, or momentary suffering for the good of others. Christianity, being designed for the good of all men, in all circumstances and conditions of life, cannot demand of man anything that would interfere with the perfection of his life, character, or true enjoyment. It is the being in a sinful world, or in a more or less sinful state, that necessitates self-sacrifice, and makes it a duty. Christ set the example of foregoing for a season all things the surrender of which would conduce to higher and more beneficent ends.

Man, in undergoing self-denial, allies himself with the Divine, and by so doing overcomes the most numerous, powerful, and subtle temptations he is exposed to. By self-sacrifice the believer in Jesus unites himself with the more immediate outgoings of the Godhead, and thus emancipates himself from the most impending, enslaving, and ruining of evils. He inbreathes immediately the love, purpose, and will of God; allies himself in destiny with the most glorious elements of being, doing, and realizing.

Self-sacrifice on behalf of others is possible only to the highest natures and most godlike of lives. It stirs in them the deepest powers, principles, realizations, and ends of existence. Self-sacrifice not only honours and blesses the self-sacrificer, it likewise benefits those who are influenced by the sacrifice, far beyond what any other deed could accomplish.

The spiritual and permanent elevation of man can never be effected by military force or communistic theories, nor by philanthropic, philosophic, scientific, literary, or artistic doings, in the national, social, or individual life of men; but only by his inbreathing the Divine, in the sacrifice of self. In the pre-christian world, when military prowess, political sagacity, moral speculation, philosophic attainment, scientific discernment, artistic skill, literary refinement, prevailed in the highest degrees, man sank in the noblest and truest of his being, life, and work. Self-sacrifice improves and benefits the outer condition of mankind, above and beyond what any other endeavour after well-being can secure. It accomplishes the truest and richest development of art, science, philosophy, government, literature, and morality. For whenever self influences man in the study or practice of these, to the full extent that it does so it perverts the endeavours of the individual to discern the true nature of things or to promote the real happiness of man. Whereas self-sacrifice, being the true exponent of the love of God, not only glorifies God, but deifies the spirit of man in the loftiest degree.

By self-sacrifice man co-operates with the Godhead in its divinest and most glorious undertaking. The teaching of revelation is that the greatest work of God is the work of saving man, and reason at once endorses the authentic dictate of revelation. As the rational, spiritual, and Divine are superior to the material, sentient, and social, so must be the re-creation of the Divine in the human. The creation of the material universe was truly a majestic deed;

the production of immortal mind and adoring spirit was a more stupendous display of power and skill, but the reclamation from a false to a true life was a greater still. To call into being, to organize and set in motion the operations of responsible spirit, was indeed a magnificent work, but to recall the same spirit from a diabolic to a Divine life, to recreate the inner chaos of free self-determining spirits, to readjust the relations, and harmonize the principles of that life, was a more majestic, a diviner work. The one required the unerring fiat of omnipotent energy going out in the conscious majesty of the Divine. The other necessitated the self-sacrifice of the Godhead, the travailing of the Incarnate One in the greatness of His strength, mighty to save, the manifestation of the sovereignty of Incarnate Love in self-sacrificing grace. As the displays of condescension are sublimer far than the manifestation of conscious power, so the rescue of man's immortal spirit from the degradation and misery of sin is greater far than the original formation of the same in the image of God.

The self-sacrifice of the sovereign is absolutely necessary to the reclamation of the rebellious. Officialism can never melt the ire of the sullen; the stubborn will does and ever will resist the command of mere authority. It is only the entreaty of compassionate self-sacrificing love that will arrest the attention, overcome the opposition, and fire with filial love and gratitude the spirit of disobedience. If the self-sacrifice of the ruler is manifested in a striking display of devotedness to the well-being of the rebellious, it will tell upon them with ready and powerful effect. God and man may lecture, threaten, denounce, and by such means endeavour to alarm the rebellious, and warn them of their danger; but the result will be only to harden them the more, and to make them more defiant. The rebel will remain in his stolid indifference, or the more violent in his wrath.

It is only by laying aside the officialism of authority, and coming before the self-willed in an unmistakable display of self-sacrifice on his behalf, that either God or man will melt the hardness of the self-willed spirit, and awake within it the risings of conviction, contrition, gratitude, love, and resolve to turn from its false and ruinous ways to the path of life and obedience. The power of self-sacrifice on behalf of the self-willed, when once perceived by them, is felt to be omnipotent in its reclaiming power to draw them into a life of devotedness. Only let the rebel spirit behold the rightful Sovereign bleeding on his behalf in the grace of self-sacrifice; let him come under the conviction that all his Sovereign's sufferings have been voluntarily undergone on his behalf, nay, inflicted by his rebel hate, on a self-sacrificing Ruler, who submits to the fierceness of ignorant enmity, that He may enable the rebel, in the light of his own doings, to see the depth of his hatred to his rightful Sovereign, and at the same time the depth of self-sacrifice which his lawful Ruler is willing to incur for his reclamation to the glory and bliss of loyal devotion; that moment he is overcome, the rebel spirit in him is slain; he is stripped of its wilfulness, and is fired in his inmost soul with the profoundest emotions of affection and delight; he is divested of his enmity, stirred in spirit, and bound to his lawful Sovereign by the most powerful and enduring bonds of filial love and fervent gratitude.*

Politics, arts, science, philosophy, morality, æsthetics, philanthropy, asceticism—notwithstanding all the earnest and persevering endeavours men have put forth through them on behalf of fallen humanity—can never of themselves raise the suffering, immoral, and sinful of

* See "Christ's Mode of Presenting Himself to the World." Book IV.

earth. And they fail to raise the fallen simply because they are unable to meet the inmost necessities of sinful and sorrowing humanity.

The benefactor of the sentient life of man can at best, by his cultivation of art, science, and literature, enable his disciple to live a more refined animal or sentient life. The benefactor of the social life of man can at best, by the cultivation and application of science to art and husbandry, trade and commerce, enable his disciple to live a more refined worldly life. The benefactor of the rational life of man can at best, by the study of philosophy, in the training of the intellectual faculties of his disciple, enable his pupil to live or luxuriate in the speculations of rationalism. The benefactor of the innate religious life of man can at best, by the cultivation of his spiritual faculties in ascetic and æsthetic endeavours, enable his disciple to live a pharisaic self-righteous life. But each and all of them can do little or nothing to elevate mankind or satisfy the deep necessities of human well-being.

These, even were they as successful as imagination can conceive, could only in a temporary manner refine and gratify a portion only of the inferior side of man's being, religion, and life. But when or where have they been successful? They cannot elevate and bless the whole life of man by quickening his inmost soul with the Divine life; and they cannot quicken his inner life, because they cannot fill the deep void, calm the secret conflict, satisfy the eager cravings, unburden the conscience, and give infallible instruction to the spirit of man. Hence revolutions, communism, socialism, nihlism, politics, ecclesiasticism, morality, commerce, philosophy, art, have never raised, and never can raise, fallen man. The experience of the pre- and post-christian worlds demonstrate this truth. The true and permanent elevation of human society is possible only through the quickening of the human soul with the Divine life. And this quickening of rebellious, fallen humanity with the life of God is possible even to God Himself only through an amazing display of the self-sacrifice of the Godhead.

The opportunities of such self-sacrifice, for either God or man, are found only in the region of the fallen. If God undertakes the elevation of fallen humanity, He must come into the sphere of sin's operations, appear before the sinner, and act in his view, so as to influence him to receive the Divine life in accordance with the principles of his nature, circumstances, necessities, and aspirations. And man, to be serviceable in the work of raising his fallen brother, must act towards him in the same manner. It is only through the self-sacrificing exertions of the elevator that the fallen can be raised.

Hence the numerous failures of the reforming institutions of mere human device. The founders and managers, instead of breathing the spirit of self-sacrifice in their discharge of the duties they have undertaken, too often display the spirit of officialism, self-assertion, and domineering, and thus produce the opposite of what is expected. Hence the necessity for the believer in Jesus, while in the world, to realize the greatness of his privileges, the grandeur of his calling, the nature of his power, and, in the spirit of self-sacrificing devotion to the glory of Christ, to copy His example. Whatever may be the opportunities of departed spirits for co-operating with the Spirit of all grace, we may be sure they will avail themselves of every occasion of doing so. Angels are ministering spirits to the heirs of salvation, and so may be departed souls. But these opportunities are as nothing to those of the believer on earth. Co-operation with the Spirit of God in self-sacrifice is only confided to the believer in Jesus in this life; and did he know his privilege, he would value it as an enviable possession. To follow Christ in the regeneration of this world is the most glorious work and highest honour conferred on man in time.

Into this region the Son of God came by His incarnation. It was the only sphere in which He could accomplish His glorious work of human redemption. And as the Scriptures represent the self-sacrifice of the Son as greater than the self-denial of the Holy Ghost, so may we regard the work of the believer in following Christ as more arduous, noble, and enviable than that of the angels or redeemed spirits in ministering to the heirs of salvation.

Did we see things now as they will be seen by us hereafter in the disclosures of the experience of the saints in glory, we should perceive that this world of sin, into which the Son of God came to win His glory, was, of all other spheres in the wide universe of being, the most favourable for winning glory and laying the deep and permanent foundations of sweetest bliss. We should see that he is the most wise and dutiful believer, who does all in his power to bring fallen immortals to Christ; we should rest in the conviction that he which "converteth a sinner from the error of his ways shall save a soul from death, and shall hide a multitude of sins." If we look at the nature of the immortal spirit of man as created in the image of God, we shall discern something of its vast and enduring capacities, responsibilities, condition, and danger. If we consider what Christ has done for the salvation of souls, if we believe in the obligation He has laid upon us to do all in our power to extend His kingdom by the conversion of sinners, if we remember the rewards He promises us, and the results of compliance with or indifference to His will, we shall perceive that our present opportunities of living for the glory of Christ are the most enviable of all privileges we could enjoy.

This was what Paul felt when he was in a strait between going to glory and bliss, or remaining in the persecutions and the sufferings of self-sacrifice in this world of sin. He was far from being indifferent to the employment, the glory, the bliss, the security, and the society of heaven, and he was no less indifferent to the persecutions, sufferings, risks, and dangers of the Christian calling on earth. He shrank from the one, and he longed for the other; yet his clear conviction of the highest glory won, and the noble rewards of the work done in the Church below through self-sacrifice, compared with the results of the work done, in the Church above, determined him to prefer remaining a longer period on earth to immediately ascending to heaven.

Self-sacrifice is not without its pains and pleasures; but the joys of the one far outmeasure and outlast the sufferings of the other. The pain is momentary and limited, the joy is boundless and enduring. The pain is like that of the woman in travail; the joy is like that of the mother embracing her man-child, and the delight with which she beholds him rising into manhood, in health, prosperity, and honour. Self is not without its gratifications, but they are only momentary and deceptive. Man ruled by self acts in accordance with the liking, thinking, and willing which are peculiar to fallen humanity, and he does so in the measure of his carnality. Self is the disease of man's spiritual life, and stands in the way of his true dignity and bliss. Self-sacrifice secures the health of the soul, and is that which dignifies and blesses the life of him who lives in it; and it is profitable to him in the measure of the true nobility of his soul.

Hence the wisdom and benignity of the Saviour in requiring every disciple coming to Him to deny himself. To deny self, an individual must struggle with and overcome his worldliness, prejudice, covetousness, devilishness, the self that is in him. In this conflict with self there is more or less pain experienced, but the pain is nothing compared with the conscious joy of overcoming self, and entering into fellowship with Jesus. Self can be overcome only as the individual yields himself up to the Spirit of God, working in him that faith which opens up to his inner eye the sublimity of the self-sacrifice of the Godhead on his behalf, and of his own on behalf of a sinful world. Self-sacrifice is the bearing of injury and wrong, that the wrongdoer may be won to rectitude, to God, and to the joy of self-sacrifice. Thus the joy of self-sacrifice far outmeasures the suffering of the self-denial it demands. The fruit of self-denial is the conscious rectitude of being and doing, the harmonious relations of life, the freedom of energy and conscious joy of fellowship with the Divine, which is the purest, deepest, and most delightful which finite being can realize. It is the joy of the Spirit, the realization of a satisfying bliss; it is the drinking of the rivers of pleasure which flow from the fount of God.

VII.

THE FOLLY OF SELFISHNESS.

CHAPTER VII.

THE FOLLY OF SELFISHNESS.

SELF is an idol, and as such is nothing in the world, or among the realities of objective existence. Still, as an idol, self exerts a fearful power in the life, and reigns with a tremendous sway over the subjective of man. The worship of self is the most degrading known to the finite, far more degrading than the worship of idols of wood, of silver, or of gold. In the homage of self, man pursues "vanities, and follows lies;" "sows to the wind, and reaps of the whirlwind." The pursuit of selfish ends must necessarily lead to disappointment; for in following these objects man only pursues the delusions of a vain imagination; he pursues things which have no existence but in the dreams of disordered minds. Self is the ignis fatuus of the world, the syren which lures man to disappointment, degradation, and woe.

The pursuit of self not only disappoints man,

but separates man from man, and turns him upon his fellows in the retaliation of imaginary and real injuries and wrongs. If men selfishly desire the same object, then will they fall out and contend about it. If the selfishness of some lead them to ensnare others, they will do an injury to the ensnared; and when the ensnared or enslaved become aroused to a sense of the wrong done to them, they will seek to escape from their bondage, and to avenge the injuries done to them by their oppressors. If the selfishness of one leads him to deceive his brother, then will he do an injury both to himself and to his brother, which when perceived by his brother will lead him to retaliate; and thus selfishness necessarily instigates those in and on whom it acts to strife and wrong-doing.

Self usurps the throne of God in the heart of man, and thus deprives man of fellowship with His Father in heaven, in the conscious enjoyment of the Divine. No human spirit can at one and the same time realize gratification in the service of self, and bliss in the consciousness of pure devotedness to God. This fact explains what appears a mystery in the experience of many professors of religion, that so few realize the pure satisfaction of spiritual joy. The explanation is that few religious professors are devoid of more or less selfishness even in their religious devotedness. There is much of self-seeking and self-pleasing in the religious acts of not a few. Some are religious, that they may escape hell, that they may procure the favour of God, and get good places in heaven. Self, in the measure in which it operates in the life of man, does and cannot but come in between the soul and the pure realizations of the Divine. The pure realization of the Divine, or sweet and satisfying fellowship with God, can be enjoyed only in and by means of the clear and full consciousness of supreme love to God, and simple devotion to His glory in the good of man.

Self necessarily involves its victims in delusive pursuits of the unattainable, and cannot but lead them in the end to disappointment, shame, sorrow, and regret in the consciousness of their defeat. Self occupying the throne of God in the heart of man must keep up in his spirit an unceasing conflict. Self must, in the measure in which it is clung to by any individual, secure the perversion of his powers, the prostitution of his faculties and capacities, and in the end the complete degradation and ruin of his life. Self, wherever it exists and acts, necessarily leads to the dishonour of God and to the injury of man.

Self not only leads to the destruction of

man's fellowship with God, in the conscious enjoyment of the Divine, but likewise as necessarily alienates man from man, sets men in opposition to one another, and leads to rivalry, disappointment, retaliation, and revenge. There is no sin or crime committed by men, but has its source in selfishness. Selfishness in its operations cannot but produce disturbance and conflict in man's nature and life. If we take the first sin as an illustration, and trace the origin of every transgression committed by man, we will find its source in self.

Self not only appears in the sentient, and works mischief in the social and religious life of man, but likewise displays its power in the speculations of his mind, and searchings after the knowledge of truth. Man has his "idola" in his philosophical speculation, as really as his "idols" in his religious life. And his idola reign with as much sovereign sway in his speculations, as his "idols" in his prejudice and superstition. Whenever self influences man, it works only for his degradation and ruin; self is a fearful tyrant in and over man. There can be no sincere friendship, brotherly love and kindness, or lasting agreement among the selfish.

Self necessarily blinds the selfish to the

perception of the first and underlying principle of all being, life, and perfection; viz., that love devotes itself to the fullest extent, and in every possible way, for the benefit of its object; that it is more blessed to give than to receive; that the Brightness of the Father's glory, who, being in the form of God, thought it no robbery to be equal with God, yet made Himself of no reputation, and took upon Himself the form of a servant, and was made in the likeness of men, and being found in fashion as a man, He humbled Himself, and became obedient to death, even the death of the cross. It also blinds man to the perception that self-sacrificing love is the only principle which sounds the deepest depths of the Godhead, and is the principle which binds all holy intelligence together, and underlies the pure bliss of all right-minded existence. It is the immutable law of well-being. The harmonizing power of the universe is, that the highest condescend to the lowest, penetrate, pervade, and fill it, and by so doing elevate it to the level of itself—the holy the unholy, the happy the suffering, the living the dead, etc.

Selfishness expelled man from Paradise, and has been the cause of all the sufferings he has since endured. Selfishness in pride leads to the miseries which man endures from the oppression of the despot on the throne to the cruelties of the despot in the family. Selfishness in the vanities of life leads to the sufferings of life which man endures in connection with his efforts to appear conspicuous and great in the highest circles and departments of fashionable life to the feeblest imitations of the frivolous and gay. Selfishness in the passions leads to the suffering man has endured from licentiousness, crime, and brutality. Selfishness in worldliness has led to the suffering man has endured from all the over-strained efforts put forth to acquire pleasure, gain position and power, and the cruelties and tyrannies he has inflicted on those he has trampled on to reach such. And selfishness has been the source of the religious abuses which have disfigured Church history, from the dispute among "the twelve," who should be the greatest, down to the proclamation of the infallibility of the Pope,—from the sectarianism of the Judaising teachers of the primitive Church to the envy and jealousy of modern times,—and in all the contentions and wranglings of the brotherhood, which have deprived them of the delights of pure spiritual life, and involved them in the heart-burnings of divisions and bitter feuds.

We cannot desire to be in a condition without moving towards it, or desire to be out of a condition without moving out of it in the degree of the intensity of the desire. Now, since selfishness is the desire of possessing and employing all being for itself, selfishness cannot realize, enjoy, or act on the principle of self-sacrifice, and must by the immutable law of existence exclude the selfish from the lofty and blessed realization of life and communion with God in the most Godlike elements of His being and doing.

If the source of conflict in the spiritual be the usurpation of self over conscience, the will of self setting itself over the Supreme will, the fallible placing itself above the Infallible; and if selfishness not only results in disobedience of the Divine, but produces strife, rivalry, envy, hatred, wrath, and revenge among the fallen, it is in the very nature of things impossible that the selfish can perceive the grandeur of the deepest underlying principle of all well-being, viz., that the Infinite condescend in self-sacrifice for the reclamation and bliss of the fallen finite, or that the selfish can believe that the loftiest condition of being and life is compliance with Christ's injunction to "love your enemies, bless them that curse you, do good to them that hate you, and pray for them which despitefully use you and persecute you."

If an enemy be one who dislikes and opposes all that is pure, lofty, and Divine in self-sacrifice, one who recklessly denounces, hates with deadly spite, imprecates vengeance on, labours to dethrone, and even put out of existence the Being who seeks to allure him from the selfish and impure to the illustrious and sublime; if cursing be the angry condemnation of the hated deeds of those that are disliked, if hatred be the opposition of the bitterest enmity to all that is held worthy of destruction, if persecution is the unavailing effort of haughty pride, to destroy and put out of existence what is essentially Divine; how can those who are under the government of such passions comply with the loftiest condition of being and life? To comply with it is difficult, nay, impossible, to the selfish, but glorious and blessed to the self-sacrificing. The principle of self-sacrifice is the embodiment of the underlying principle of the incarnation, life, death, resurrection, and ascension of the Son of God. The end for which the Logos left the bosom of the Father, and came into this world of sin, was to manifest in Himself, through suffering in the material, this divinest principle of being and life.

Self moves in selfishness, it can move in nothing else; and in moving in selfishness it acts in opposition to all the interests of universal well-being, the interests of the spirit in which it reigns, as of the individuals it opposes; and in so acting it arouses the antagonism of those it would oppress, and its own exasperation at being resisted. The law of self-defence is as primary as the law of self-aggression and exasperation. Self, by moving in selfishness, kindles the fires of its own tormenting, forges the fetters of its own bondage, builds the walls of its own prison, immures itself in its own dungeon, voluntarily goes into a bondage out of which it cannot, do what it will, raise itself. Self-escape by its own efforts from the grasp of selfishness is in the nature of things an utter impossibility; self cannot reform itself, or be improved by others; it will not yield; it can only be annihilated by a superior power; and the only power that can annihilate self is the condescension of self-sacrifice on behalf of the voluntary victims of selfishness.

If selfishness necessarily shut out from the perception, participation, and enjoyment of the consciousness of such being and life, if it set immortal beings in mortal strife with one another, if it fire the soul with the most tormenting passions, if it plunge its dupes into the lowest degradation, and hold them in the most galling bondage, surely selfishness is the greatest of human follies.

Of the evil nature and baneful character of selfishness, mankind might long ere now have been well informed. But man, with all his opportunities and means of knowing the tremendous power of selfishness, believes not in its devilishness. It may therefore be necessary, in the wise over-rulings of a gracious Providence, to permit such a display of its true nature and workings as will exhibit its tremendous evil so as to open the eyes of men to its real character And if we mistake not, the present aspect of the civilized world indicates the approach of such an event. The civilized world is at this moment honey-combed with Socialism, Communism, and Nihilism, to such an extent, that if God does not restrain them, they will so unite and combine as to display their true workings in such a manner as will astonish the world, and convince men that selfishness is nothing but essential evil, and thus prepare them for the reception of self-sacrifice as the only principle of well-being in a fallen race.

VIII.

THE EFFICIENT PRINCIPLE OF CHRISTIAN LIFE.

CHAPTER VIII.

THE EFFICIENT PRINCIPLE OF CHRISTIAN LIFE.

IT is in the spiritual that man lives and realizes his being. The spiritual is the underlying principle of all human existence. The spiritual dwells in and realizes itself in the legal, the legal dwells in and manifests itself in the formal, the formal dwells in and displays itself in the material. Matter is the spoken or written language of thought, the gossamer web of life, that through which spirit holds fellowship with spirit, the Infinite with the finite, and the finite with the finite. The material is the conditioning of the spiritual.

The Christian is to distinguish between the nature and the disease of the life of enmity, and while he is to dread and shun the one, he is to love and desire the well-being of the other. He is to perceive that his enemy is capable of becoming as deified in his life as he is Divine in his nature; that the very existence of enmity implies the capability of the divine loving of life, the transformation of the inner character of his spirit, and that the work of transforming a spirit from the devilish to the Divine is the grandest achievement possible either to finite or infinite self-sacrifice. He is to desire and design this possible transformation. He is meekly and patiently to submit to and bear with the opposition of enmity in the spirit of self-sacrifice; and supplicating the aid of omnipotent grace, that he may allure his enemy to this nobler and more sublime existence; trusting in the conscious superiority of the meekness of self-sacrifice to the meanness of self-seeking, he is to be confident of the success of his endeavour. The one is not for a moment to stand in comparison with the other.

Love is the supreme, all-glorious blessing of being. "God is love." We distinguish between the nature of humanity which is to love, and its disease which is enmity. Love realizes itself in the embrace of its objects. It cannot realize its fulness while alone. Love without an object would be a contradiction in nature. The intenser the love, the sweeter, more powerful, and benevolent the life. The more underserving the object of love, the more divine the passion that embraces it. The greater the suffering, degradation, and helplessness from which love rescues, the deeper the realization of the rescuer and the rescued.

Love disclosing its inmost depths in self-sacrifice for the glory and bliss of its enemies, is the most sublime of all possible revelations of the Divine condescension of the powerful and happy on behalf of the helpless and the suffering. Such is the true outcome of love in its manifestations. It is the true enjoyment of love in the realization of itself. It is the genuine reward of love in the triumph of its self-sacrifice. It is love proving itself superior to enmity.

The mission of the Logos is the revelation of the deep things of God. God having begun to manifest Himself, could not consistently stop short of a revelation of His inmost Being. Christianity has its foundation in the inmost recesses of the Godhead. Hence it is "the gathering together of all things in Christ." It is the efficient preparation for God being all in all.

And thus the manifestation of the principle of self-sacrifice is the inevitable condition or result of God's revelation of Himself. Love being essentially active, it must manifest itself; love being essentially gracious, it must display its yearnings; love being essentially self-sacrificing, it must adopt every possible means of realizing itself in the fulness of its disclosure. Love, while alienation and suffering continues, will leave no effort untried to rescue its objects from the dominion of evil. The self-sacrifice of love shows that the purest, sweetest, and most enduring bliss is possible only in the fellowship of love.

Christ not only inculcated such a principle, but exemplified it in His mission. He came from the realms of bliss into this world of sin and suffering, on an embassy of mercy, to overcome the principalities of evil, that He might prove His own and His Father's love to our guilty race, and give the fullest evidence that the Godhead's highest, most cherished desire was the rescue of sinners from sin, through the display of self-sacrifice on their behalf; and in this He bequeathed His legacy to His Church.

Christ receives His disciples into the consciousness of God's unselfish self-sacrificing love to man, and of the unselfish self-sacrificing love of man to God, and to his fellow-men. This love is one, and so is the consciousness of it, and thus it is that "he that dwelleth in love dwelleth in God, and God in him." And thus disciples received into this consciousness are made partakers of the Divine nature and life. There is in Christ, in the life which is through Him, if we may use the phrase, a "pantheism" of life. The disciples of Christ are enabled to see into the reality and glory of the self-sacrificing love of God, and are drawn into the fellowship of this love, which is the highest, noblest, sweetest realization of conscious being.

The realization of love is the grandest, most influential, and enduring form of being. "God is love." Love takes possession of the deepest capacities, the highest powers, the noblest desires of existence. Love is vivid delight in the contemplation of its objects, and untiring devotion to their good. Love is self-rewarding. It loves not for the bliss of loving, but is blessed because it realizes itself in its activity on behalf of its objects. Love cannot be selfish; selfishness is contrary to its nature, and suicidal to its enjoyment. Love is blessed, because it is love, and because it loves. It lives in bliss, because it delights in the blessedness of its objects, and realizes most of itself in its endeavours to secure to them the highest amount of pure enjoyment. Hence love is self-sacrificing. The danger, degradation, and distress of its objects awake its deepest emotions, arouse its tenderest yearnings, impel it into every possible exertion on their behalf, and make it impatient till it embrace them in its own loveliness and joy, and behold them in possession of its very image and life.

Never was love more itself than when in blood and agony it hung upon the accursed tree, and expressed itself in the self-sacrifice of the cross. Love never had a beginning, and it will never have an end. Love is uncreated, self-existent, omnipotent, eternal. Although, in the mysteries of time, hatred has sprung into existence to dispute the reign of love, love through self-sacrifice has conquered hatred, and in the unfoldings of its own omnipotent loveliness must prevail over all the ingenuity and wiles of hatred. The radiant light of love, the pure bliss of love, the omnipotent power of love, the self-sacrificing grace of love, must chase away all the darkness, and rise superior to all the degradation and woe of hatred, in all who yield to its invading force, and open their hearts to its indwelling operations. No finite mind can conceive what is implied in Christ's receiving His disciples into the consciousness of His self-sacrificing love. In the love of God, man is nearest to God. He is in life one with God, and must be for ever with Him. Is love less a reality in being than the qualities or affinities of matter? are its operations less important? or is it less scientific to trace the nature and results of its movements?

Love is grateful, admiring, adoring, assimilating in its actions. It vivifies, strengthens, blesses itself in feeding on the self-sacrificing of its Divinity. In the disciples of Jesus it transforms itself into the very image of its adoration and delight, as it gratefully recognizes the favours the Master confers on all His friends. It lives in the life as it rises in the consciousness of a oneness with its object. So conscious is love of its own Divinity, so satisfied is love with itself, so convinced is love of its own superiority, glory, and bliss, that it can rest in nothing short of its objects being transformed into the full consciousness of its life; and so adoring is love, that it can be satisfied with nothing short of conscious oneness with its object. The Father so loves the Son, that nothing short of the bringing out into the brightest radiance the inner perfections of His being and life would satisfy the Father's heart. And the Son so loved the Father's will, that to give the highest possible proof of His disinterested devotedness to that will He laid down His life. And the Father so loves the human as lived by Christ, that to raise all such humanity to unity of consciousness, a oneness of life in glory and joy with Christ, in His reign over all, is the only end that can satisfy the cherished yearnings of His gracious love. And humanity in Christ is so devoted to the glory of the Father in the Son, that nothing short of the realization of this goal of life will afford it rest, and satisfy its joy.

The objects, the exertions, the principles, the motives of love in self-sacrifice are necessary to display its true nature and Divine character; and in such deeds love lives and luxuriates. The objects for whose benefit it exerts itself to the highest conceivable degree are the undeserving, suspicious, rebellious foes, who treat it with contemptuous scorn; and for the glory and blessedness of these it exerts itself in every possible manner, and to the utmost extent. In so exerting itself, its motives and principles of action are to do nothing but what is in the strictest accordance with equity and right in enduring and endeavouring to the very utmost of self-sacrifice. Its motives are to disclose itself to its foes by voluntary endurance, on their behalf, of the wrongs they inflict upon it, until by its patient bearing it shall overcome their enmity, quicken them with its own spirit, and draw them into the realization of its own fellowship and inmost consciousness of the dignity and joy of self-sacrificing devotedness. To breathe the spirit of this love, to live in the imitation of this devotedness, to realize in human consciousness this Divine life of self-sacrificing love, is to know Christ in the power of His death, and to enter into conscious participation of the motives, principles, and ends of the self-sacrificing life of fellowship with Him.

Jesus, in raising His disciples into the realization of this fellowship with Himself, raises them into the consciousness of swaying with Him the one sceptre, wielding with Him His own power. In this self-sacrificing devotedness to human well-being in the promotion of His glory, while exulting in spending and being spent in exhibiting Christ to the view of the world, in order to draw it into faith in Jesus, the disciple necessarily exerts the influence of His saving power, and in the conscious exertion of such power he as necessarily reigns with Him, as he sits with Him on His throne. Christ's disciples, living thus, cannot but feel that they live in a conscious oneness with Him in His self-sacrificing devotedness to the salvation of a world lying under sin. In so living, they cannot but breathe somewhat of quickening, enlightening, and elevating power into the immortal spirit of man, and thus prove themselves one with Christ in the fellowship of His reign.

This reign of self-sacrificing devotedness displays itself in the truest forms of loveliness in lifting immortal souls out of the bondage of evil by introducing them into the realization of the Divine. In the measure in which Christ makes His disciples the agents of quickening undying souls with the Divine life, of enlightening immortal minds with the knowledge of the truth, of retracing His image on the substance of humanity, in drawing men into the fellowship of self-sacrificing devotedness to the glory of God, He raises them up to sit with Him on His throne, shares with them His sceptre, gives them to realize a conscious oneness with Himself, enables them to rejoice with Him in the advance of His reign.

Such is the nature of self-sacrifice, and such is the condescension of the Divine, that there is no ray of its glory which Christ will not bestow, no element of its bliss which He will not impart. Thus Christ frequently spoke to His disciples of their sharing with Him His glory, and of His joy remaining in them. Addressing His Father on their behalf, He said, "The glory which Thou gavest Me I have given them." If we enquire into the nature of this gift, we shall perceive that it consists in employing them in the advance of His kingdom, and thus sharing with them His reign.

As they share with Him in His self-sacrifice, so they reign with Him in a oneness of nature, life, intercourse, destiny, and duration. As they reign with Him in a oneness of conscious love, in a oneness of the realization of the Divine, in a oneness of the manifestation of the true, in a oneness of dominion over all evil, so they realize with Him a oneness of the conscious consummation of His glory and bliss. As He ascended to His native skies, and shed down upon "the eleven" His Spirit, they began to discern something of the true self-sacrificing spirit of His reign, something of the radiance of His glory, and of the sweetness of His heavenly bliss; in one word, something of the graciousness of the Christian calling. And the zeal of consecrating themselves in self-sacrificing devotedness as His agents and instruments in establishing His kingdom of grace in the world, began to glow in their spirits, so that from that time forth the honour of being the immediate followers of the self-sacrificing Immanuel, in establishing and extending His dominion over all principalities and powers, became with them the ruling passion, the absorbing thought, and the governing power of their lives.

What Christ bestowed immediately on "the eleven," He holds out for the reception of all who believe in Him, and secures to them according to the measure of their faith in Him, in their realization of the Divine, their devotion to, or readiness to act on, the principle of self-sacrifice. And all that He does Himself and by His disciples in the maintenance of principle and in defence of right, is in strict accordance with law. He raises out of the bondage of the law of sin and death, into the realization of the freedom of the law of life, all who give themselves up to the principle of His life and death.

Prior to Christ's death, "the eleven" did not know Him. They had but imperfect conceptions of His nature, dim glimpses of the true dignity of His person, and of the object of His mission. They had no apprehension of His character, or discernment of His work. No, they had no idea of His incarnate personality, of the tenderness of His Divine love, of the condescending depths of His self-sacrifice, of the vastness of, His eternal design, of the wisdom of His infinite plan, of the glory of His gracious kingdom, or the bliss of the fellowship of His endless reign. No, not even in their most sanguine dreams or vivid conceptions of His coming glory, did they see into the grandeur of His work or the wonder of His love. But the stirring events of the garden and the cross, read by them in the light of His resurrection and return to them in the fulness of His grace, poured such a flood of light into their benighted minds, as to open their eyes to the past and the present of His sayings and doings, as to afford them new views of His kingdom, and of themselves. They could now by the glance of a moment learn of Him what former years had failed to teach them. Thomas had only to see the print of the nails and the mark of the spear, to be constrained to exclaim, "My Lord and my God." Now that they gazed upon Him, the risen One, they could yield their understanding up to the flooding light He poured into their minds, as He opened to them the Scripture concerning Himself. Beginning with Moses, and ending with Malachi, He showed them that the end of the Scriptures was to testify of Him as the Messiah, that by the sacrifice of Himself He should save the race.

And now that they no longer beheld Him as a political Messiah, but as the Son of God come to found a spiritual kingdom which was to embrace the regenerate of all time and place, they began to perceive that to realize His life, aid in His undertaking, enjoy His fellowship, and reign with Him in His spiritual kingdom, was an honour, the thought of which they fondly cherished in their hearts. To be one with Him in the spiritual they now began to see was the highest glory and purest bliss to which the spirit of man could aspire. The experience of "the eleven" is an illustration of the transition of the Church from the old to the new dispensation of the epoch she and her disciples have to pass through. For what He was to "the eleven," He is to all who believe in Him, and He is so in the simplicity and strength of their faith.

The substance of what we have said is, that the great difficulty of raising the believer and the Church to the highest conditions of the Divine life is the slowness of man to learn the things of God, and to learn that there are no limitations in God. Love will maintain the operations of law, especially in the higher regions of life. God creates substances, in which He places principles, powers, capacities, relations, laws, for the enjoyment of personal life. Over these He sets intelligence, conscience, will ; *i.e.*, personality to preserve and develop these in harmony for progress in well-being. And to the free agent He gives the power of choice, that he may judge and act in the consciousness of his personal freedom, in the preservation of his life, and harmony of relationship in the enjoyment of dignity and bliss, but so as to suffer in degrading himself, if by selfish action he disturbs the harmony of his being and relationship.

Love recognizes the principles of retribution, has satisfaction in justice, maintains and defends the harmonious operations of nature, and upholds the necessary functions of life. It is love that has produced these, placed them in their several relations, set them in their harmonious operations, and delights in seeing them developing their capabilities. Love has produced them to realize conscious dignity and bliss in harmonious operation, and suffering in a sense of degradation and shame, in a condition of discord. And love cannot go back on her own work, and destroy or alter the nature or capacities of these, when they by an act of personal disobedience are brought into a state of discord.

Love cannot delight in suffering for its own sake; were she to do so, she would be guilty of deep sin, and realize inner conflict, degradation, and woe. Neither can love delight in the conflict of nature and life that produce the suffering; and much less can she delight in the disobedience or act of self-will which produces the conflict. Love is all-comprehensive in her discernment and appreciation of the relations and operations of varied existence, in their harmonious development. She is also impartial in her attachments and yearnings. Love cannot sacrifice a higher for an inferior object or end. That would be for love, in her all-wise discerning, to act unjustly, unwisely, unbenignly, which is an utter impossibility.

Love never requires to be appeased towards the objects of her affections; if she did, she would act contrary to her inmost nature and essential impulses. When she sees the objects of affection suffering, she must hasten herself to draw them out of their suffering, out of their conflict, out of their disobedience, out of their self-willedness or selfishness; and in all this she acts spontaneously, in accordance with her inmost nature.

Love never needs the interference of another to awaken her sympathies; were she to do so, she would not be love; in doing so she would be guilty of the inconsistency of doing a wrong to herself, of producing a conflict in her inmost self, of committing self-destruction. The very supposition that love could require the interference of another is an injury, a wrong, an insult to love.

Love shows mercy in long-suffering, and

creates of herself the remedy for the evil she mourns and longs to draw men out of. Love cannot look on suffering, conflict, disobedience, self-willedness, or selfishness, with indifference. Love must yearn to rescue the suffering from their conflict of nature, from their disobedient obstinacy, their self-willed rebelliousness, their selfishness; and in so doing she must act in accordance with the principles, powers, capabilities, and relations of universal existence.

Love displays her inmost nature, and exerts her greatest power, in self-sacrifice. Self-sacrifice is the manifestation of the deepest, most worthy, and expressive deed of love. It is in the manifestation of self-sacrifice that love acts most gloriously, in the display of self-sacrifice on man's behalf, that the Godhead has created the power which above every other is most capable of destroying the rebel principle of fallen life.

Love with tears of blood entreats the self-willed, the disobedient, the conflicting, the suffering, to fall into her embrace. Self-will is the rebel principle of fallen life, the only gulph between man and God. Self-willedness is the most ruinous, unjust, and unsatisfactory condition of existence possible to finite intelligence. Self-sacrificing love must yearn to draw the rebellious out of such a condition of life. The mother never so fully and correctly expresses herself as when she rushes into imminent danger to snatch her child from its devouring jaw. And the wife is most the Christian lady, when it may be in rags she toils to the utmost of her ability to feed and clothe her children, does what she can to make her home as comfortable as it is in her power to do, and sits to midnight hours to receive with meek and gentle smiles her inebriate husband, setting before him the morsel she has withheld from her own lips, that she may win him to God and to virtue.

The sinner, by believing in the self-sacrificing love of God on his behalf, realizes its powerful operations in his soul, quickening him with its own consciousness. The power of self-sacrifice once apprehended cannot be resisted; hence the believer in the self-sacrificing love of God on his behalf cannot but realize its transforming operations. The only hindrance to a sinner's salvation is his resistance of the Spirit striving to work faith in him.

The believer in God's Son is thus saved from selfishness, self-will, disobedience, conflict, and suffering, by faith. He sees the character of these things, and detests them, as in the light of the cross he sees them causing the self-sacrifice of God's Son. The believer cannot but glow with love, gratitude, confidence, and delight in God as the gracious Self-sacrificer. And thus the believer in God's Son must be the most godlike of finite existence.

We thus see the fitness of Christ or the adaptation of His work to glorify God in the salvation of man. It brings into clear view the deepest depths, the inmost recesses of love. It displays the only manifestation of the Divine that can slay the enmity of the "carnal mind." It recreates the sinner in the life of God, by enabling him to see into the breadth and length, the depth and height of the love of God, so as to be filled with all the fulness of God. Love is the fulfilling of the law, *i.e.*, the securing of the end of all legal or legitimate existence. It alone realizes the requirements of the highest ends of finite or infinite being.

IX.

IS A ONENESS OF LIFE POSSIBLE TO THE FINITE WITH THE INFINITE, AND OF THE INFINITE WITH THE FINITE?

CHAPTER IX.

IS A ONENESS OF LIFE POSSIBLE TO THE FINITE WITH THE INFINITE, AND OF THE INFINITE WITH THE FINITE?

IT is now generally regarded as an established point in controversial matters, nay, has even come to be looked upon as an axiomatic truth, that no school in philosophy or sect in religion will exist for any given time, that has not some element of truth to sustain it; wherever an element of truth is found, although blended with much error, it will preserve its school or sect from annihilation, and sooner or later manifest itself in its true form.

To endeavour to establish a pantheistic doctrine in one phase or another has been the aim of philosophic effort and devout feeling from the earliest ages to the present time. There seems ever to have been among the highest intellects and most fervent hearts of earth some who have given themselves persistently to the endeavour to secure a basis for their ideal visions of a pantheistic doctrine, and ardent piety in its sublimest flights has sighed to burst asunder the bands of the finite, that it might catch a glimpse of the Infinite, and lose itself in the feeblest of its sparks.

Is this pantheistic dream one of the many penalties which man has had to pay for yielding to the temptation, "Ye shall be as gods"? or is it the feeble stirring of an irrepressible instinct of the human spirit, impelling man onward to the goal of his destiny? In other words, was man's first sin a misdirected impatience or false impulse of an indestructible yearning to surmount the limits of finite consciousness by an immediate realization of the fulness of communion with the Infinite life? If there had not been a desire grounded in a felt capacity for immediate communion with the Infinite in man's spirit, there could have been no temptation in the promise, "Ye shall be as gods." It could not have been for man a snare—however artfully laid—to entice him to lose his satisfying bliss in a progressive learning and enlarging fellowship with God, by a rash and unguarded attempt to grasp the end of his existence in an impatient, instantaneous seizure.

Man is ever striving to regain his lost liberty and power in an endeavour to rise superior to the evil under which he groans, by the hope that in the conscious enjoyment of all his desire he may attain to the possession of his "chief good." The one effort of his soul seems to be to burst the trammels of his finite surroundings by entering into union with the Infinite and Eternal. He may in the dissolution of his mortal frame surmount the sense by which he is at present ensphered, he may even surmount his intellectual visions, as Paul obviously did in the "third heaven," if it be an unquestionable truth that "realization in soul" is possible without, and superior to, mere discernment of intellect.

A pantheism of matter is inconceivable, whether matter be regarded as the reverse of spirit, or the gossamer web of spirit's fabricating. A pantheism of personalities is still more inconceivable, inasmuch as personality is that which distinguishes and holds itself apart from all other entities. A pantheism of the highest order of life is the only pantheism conceivable to man; and on this profoundest of all themes of pantheism, Christianity seems to throw a flood of light. Christ in this, as in every other aspect of human want, is the "desire of all nations;" in Himself, His work, His teaching, He is the "all in all," He is the supreme love of the Infinite,

Eternal, and Divine, He is the only condition of human well-being. His revelation is, "He that dwelleth in love dwelleth in God, and God in him;" that the pure supreme love of the Divine enables its possessor to comprehend the incomprehensible, so as to be filled with all the fulness of God; that faith in Him, in its endless transformations, secures for the believer a oneness of life with His, brings the Infinite into the finite by assimilating the finite into a oneness with the Infinite, and thus shows us that in a oneness of spirit, *i.e.*, of love, mind, and life, we realize a pantheism of soul.

There are mysteries in God, in being, in life, in man, in providence, in Christianity; but these mysteries are not contradictions; they are the conditions of the profounder relations of truth: to the uninitiated they are so profound as to be incomprehensible, but to the Omniscient they are clear; in His consciousness of Himself, and in His discernment of the external, He has given existence out of and beyond Himself. And to men He has given the capacity for endless progress in knowledge. The solution of these mysteries is ever opening up in the enlargement of their capability for the reception and enjoyment of Him as the portion of their souls. But can God impart Himself fully to mere capacity, to mere spirit, to mere life or consciousness? Can He impart Himself in all His fulness—*i.e.*, in the fulness of Him who filleth all in all—to anything short of the consciousness of self-sacrificing love in its devotedness to the well-being of enemies? This may be the profoundest question possible to man.

The manifestation of the perfection of nature and life may be possible only through suffering. Is it not in the display of this truth that the Captain of salvation was made perfect through suffering? And certainly in exposing themselves to death by relieving the suffering in the pestilence from which the heathen fled, the early Christians won the applause of the idolaters themselves. In the discipline of personal, family, social, and national life, man reaches the heights of perfection. The martyr at the stake has won admiration in the display of heavenly graces, and reached the heights of the Divine. The attainment of the highest perfection through suffering may be involved in the very nature of being. If the Incarnate Revealer of the inner depths of Godhead required to pass through the ordeal of the severest suffering in order to His realization of the highest perfection possible to Him, was there not a deep necessity for such suffering? And this necessity lay not in a fiction or a freak of the Infinite mind, but in the deepest depths of the uncreated essence.

There can be no enjoyment of life outside of the consciousness of life ; if such there could be, where would it be found ? Is not consciousness the sphere, measure, condition of life ? If enjoyment could be found outside of consciousness, body might exist outside of space. Satisfaction in action must be within the contemplation or conscious performance of the action. There can be no satisfaction of doing what is not done. If there could, when or in what way could it be realized ? If we could conceive of the possibility of such, our nature would be in itself a contradiction. Spirit which is essentially active cannot exist but in a state of activity. If it could, it must exist outside of itself. It would exist contrary to its essential nature. It would exist where and when it did not exist. Action cannot be without manifesting itself in internal consciousness or external form. We cannot think or will without knowing that we do so. We cannot will without moving in volition, and we cannot move in volition without realizing a change in consciousness. The subjective is necessary to the objective, and the objective to the subjective. There can be no idea without mind, or mind without idea. The relation between mind and thought is necessary, immutable, enduring, and so of spirit and consciousness. Love cannot exist but in loving. Love must thus have a proper object of its love. Thus there must be a plurality in the Godhead, or God would be selfish, loving only Himself, and creation would never have been, self-sacrifice never known, the deepest possibility of life latent, and the ultimate principle of being undisclosed.

The Absolute must *clearly, fully, perfectly* know Himself. There can be no shade of darkness dimming the all-seeing glance of the omniscient eye: all things are and must be naked and open to the eyes of Him with whom we have to do. And if so with being external to Him, how much more so with His own inmost consciousness. The Absolute must also fully enjoy Himself. If there could be any obstacle or marring element to the enjoyment of His own being in the Absolute, He could not be the absolutely perfect One. If there could be any external restraint or condition to the enjoyment of the Absolute, He could not be such. The Absolute is without conditions, consequently without limitations of any kind.

Could Eternal Love realize Himself otherwise than through self-sacrifice? Is love realized outside of the consciousness that measures it? and does it measure itself until it undergoes self-sacrifice on behalf of its objects? Love does not sound its depths until in the struggle of self-sacrifice the mother yields her darling to the grasp of death; nor does it do so in the father's heart until in anguish of spirit he exclaims, "Would God I had died for thee, my son, my son!" It was in this that David was the man after God's heart. Hence Christ says, (John x. 17, 18,) "Therefore doth my Father love me, because I lay down my life, that I might take it again. No man taketh it from me, but I lay it down of myself. I have power to lay it down, and I have power to take it again. This commandment have I received of my Father."

Thus love surmounts and surpasses intellect in the depth and comprehensiveness of its discernment. Self-sacrificing love penetrates the deepest mysteries of being and life, knows as only the Godhead Itself can know. Hence the profundity of Paul's prayer on behalf of the Ephesian Church, "That He would grant you, according to the riches of His glory, to be strengthened with might by His Spirit in the inner man; that Christ may dwell in your hearts by faith; that ye, being rooted and grounded in love, may be able to comprehend with all saints what is the breadth, and length, and depth, and height; and to know the love of Christ, which passeth knowledge, that ye might be filled with all the fulness of God." In this wonderful passage we have the teaching that the penetration of love far excels the ken of intellect. Hence the class of passages which direct our attention to the texts which dwell on the superiority and power of love to intellect. The realization of Himself in the conscious perfection of His being and doing is the joy of God's self-sacrifice. This reward is not that for which the Godhead resolved to enter into self-sacrifice; but that which inevitably arises out of the Godhead sacrificing Itself. The attainment of this realization was not and could not be the end of God's self-sacrifice. Self-sacrifice cannot be for any personal end or gain; self-sacrifice must be for the benefit of beloved ones. Had God manifested Himself in sacrifice for His own gain or benefit, He would have acted from selfishness, and would not have displayed self-sacrificing devotedness. Selfishness is the very opposite of self-sacrifice. The one necessarily excludes the other. Working for selfish ends is utterly impossible to self-sacrifice. Suffering may be involved in the very nature of the highest life, and may be the necessary medium of its purest enjoyment, and yet is and must be the abnormal state of that life. It must thus be only momentary, or the brief passage through which life enters into the full realization of itself.

If such be the case, Christianity is not an after-thought of the Godhead, but the outcome of the deepest conception of the Infinite mind, the manifestation of the underlying principle of all profound life. God is love, and love realizes its depth and fulness, its sweetest and most satisfying joy, through self-sacrifice on behalf of its objects. The pure joy of unselfish self-sacrificing love in devotion to the highest well-being of its beloved offspring far transcends the momentary pang of suffering on their behalf; and thus it is that in the conscious suffering of self-sacrifice there is realized the sweetest satisfaction and delight.

Self-sacrifice is the only avenue through which life can enter into its loftiest consciousness, its richest realization, its purest enjoyments. The refusal, then, to realize self-sacrifice necessarily excludes from the highest realm of conscious life and enjoyment; and in this lies the deep significance of what is mentioned in the Hebrews: "We see Jesus, who was made a little lower than the angels for the suffering of death, crowned with glory and honour, that He by the grace of God should taste death for every man: for it became Him for whom are all things, and by whom are all things, in bringing many sons unto glory, to make the Captain of their salvation perfect through suffering." "For in the days of His flesh, when He had offered up prayers and supplications, with strong crying and tears, unto Him that was able to save Him from death, and was heard in that He feared." "Though He was a Son, yet learned He obedience by the things which He suffered;" *i.e.*, by self-sacrifice He entered into the condition of fullest consciousness, power, and beneficence.

The possibility of self-sacrifice may thus be the underlying principle of the Godhead. The Logos who dwelt in the inner depths of the Absolute Essence, descended through self-denial and self-sacrifice to the lowest possible depths of condescension, that He might realize and manifest the fulness of the Godhead, and thus allure a rebel race into an ascent with Him to the highest possible heights of glory and bliss the purest enjoyment of all the fulness of the Infinite and Eternal, which may be the only possession which can reclaim and retain the beings created in the image of God, in free and perfect allegiance to the Absolute in the revelation of Himself, and afford them that communion with the Infinite and Eternal which will make them as gods. Here, doubtless, are mysteries, but mysteries which will arrest and rivet adoring powers of all loyal intelligence throughout the endless ages of conscious life. As the simple law of gravitation holds the architecture of the material universe in its glorious order, so will the principle of self-sacrifice be the power by which the Son will bring back the kingdom to God the Father, and bind in the grandeur of God's finished work "all things in Christ which are in heaven and which are on earth."

If love cannot fully realize itself in mere loving, but only in self-sacrifice on behalf of its objects, and thus enable them to enter into the loftiest fellowship with itself, might not love for the highest ends of life permit a transition of spiritual consciousness out of love into enmity? We know that spirit in the mysterious possibilities of its consciousness may pass from a state of ardent affection into one of bitter hatred. How often is this made apparent in human experience!

There are disintegrating operations among the forces of being and phases of life. Such operations destroy not the substances, principalities, powers, or personalities of life, but in the emotions, feelings, desires and aims of life they make fearful havoc. This disintegrating power is selfishness. Selfishness is regardless of everything but its own gratification through the pursuit of its own ends, by its own means, in its own way. In the wars and persecutions of earth it displays most of itself. Sin has no substantive existence. It is only an abnormal condition of life, a disease of personality, a burning fever of enmity in the breast of the rebellious. It effaces the image of God from the soul of man, deprives him of the sense of the worthiness of his life, the consciousness of the rectitude of his being and doing, and brings on him the condemnation of conscience. It involves him in restlessness, subjects him to struggle and conflict, and leads him to attempt his justification by any and every possible effort. It fires him with aversion to all that stands in the way of his endeavours to vindicate himself and secure the object of his desires.

A close attention to what passes within when we are under the influence of temptation may afford an obscure conception of how man fell. We know that if we dwell on the contemplation of the forbidden, we realize a growth of the desire to do what we fear to be wrong or doubt to be right; or if we endeavour to rid ourselves of the sense of wrong-doing by an attempt to palliate or vindicate what we have done, there rises within us a vindictive feeling towards whatever would press home upon us the conviction of transgression. In this consciousness we may obtain a vague idea of how a spirit under an impatient desire of realizing the fulness of its life might have been induced in a hasty deed to transgress the law of its well-being, and to turn against whatever would press upon it the conviction that it had violated the condition of holy realization. And thus, however inadequately, we may conceive how sin invaded the fair creation of God. But how the temptation arose, which inclined man to such an act, is beyond our imagination to conceive.

Sin lays on God the necessity of maintaining in conflict the powers which it has brought into a state of disturbance. God cannot suspend the operations, or annihilate these powers which sin has disturbed, immediately they are brought into a state of conflict. He must inflict the penalty of the broken law by upholding in conflict the powers which act in disturbance, while the combination endures in which they operate. And the sinner is utterly helpless to deliver himself from any or all the consequences of his sin. Creation can furnish no power adequate to readjust the relations of life disturbed by sin. This must be a power capable of harmonizing the relations, of alluring the love, of awakening the gratitude, and consecrating the life of the repentant sinner; in other words, of readjusting the principles of man's life, of drawing his spirit into delightful communion with God, of alluring his heart into union with the law, administration, and powers of Heaven. Hence sin is the most awful evil possible to man. It is in him defiance and antagonism to God. It was not permitted for its own sake, but that occasion might be taken from it of securing the one true end of all existence.

If Divine love essentially contain in it the element of self-sacrifice, the love of enemies, the yearning to embrace through self-sacrifice its bitterest foes; if while it could never influence to wrong in any way, or encourage to sin in any degree, it might for the higher ends of being permit the self-will of selfishness to display itself in fiendish violence, thereupon taking the opportunity of bearing the enmity of sin in such a display of its devotion to the well-being of the sinner, as shall overcome his hatred and fire him with the love that can raise him to the fullest realization of its Divine emotions, elevate him to the loftiest altitude of life by enabling him to discern the inmost recesses of love displaying itself in stooping to self-sacrifice for the rescue of others; was it in any way inconsistent with love thus to act?

There is going on in humanity a regenerating, vitalizing transformation of life, by means of the Infinite descending into the finite, the Divine into the human. And this is in accordance with the underlying principle of all existence, the accomplishment of the grandest achievement of the Divine acting along with the human. The mode of renewing and elevating consists in the higher descending into the lower life, and by so doing transforming its state into a higher condition. In this operation of underlying principle we perceive the workings of the inmost power of the uncreated essence. It would appear that only thus could the inmost depths of the gracious be disclosed.

And as with the Infinite, so with the finite Christian life. The renewed, the joyous, the rich, must descend to the poor, the corrupt, the sad; the civilized, the learned, the virtuous, to the savage, the ignorant, the vicious; the meek, the benignant, the loving, to the haughty, revengeful, hating.

If, in the mysteries of love and the condescension of grace, the rebel victim of self is enabled to see the Sovereign of all drenched in blood by and for his emancipation from the bondage of self, then self in him is destroyed, his selfishness is annihilated. He sees the wondrous condescension of self-sacrifice, he realizes in its elevating power its transforming operations; he is now no longer the rebellious prodigal, but the filial son. The vision of the Godhead stooping in self-sacrifice for the life of the suicidal child, overwhelms him with love, gratitude, and self-sacrificing devotedness. The Eternal Spirit entering into and taking up His abode, in quickening grace expels all rebellious dispositions, fires him with the purest emotions of glowing love. And if his quickened spirit is guided aright in the direction of self-sacrificing devotion to universal well-being, he enters upon the most glorious, blessed, and beneficent life possible, the rising into the heavenly, the assimilation of the Divine, the deepening consciousness of the True, the fullest, sweetest, most transforming communion of the finite with the Infinite.

In these operations of self-sacrificing love we see the gathering together of all things in Christ, the putting down of all insubordinate rule, authority, and power, the delivering up of the kingdom to the Father, that God may be all in all, the losing of the consciousness of the imperfection of the selfish finite in the realization of unselfish communion with the Infinite, the loss of the selfish fallen in the enjoyment of the renewed, the realization of the self-sacrificing life of God in the consecration of the self-sacrificing life of man. This is the absorption of the human by the Divine for which the mystic longs, the pantheism after which the philosopher enquires.

Was it then unworthy of God, in the mysterious conditioning of the Absolute, the revealing of the deep things of the True, the manifesting of the inner depths of self-sacrifice, in the display of the transforming power of Eternal Love, that its objects might be raised into its purest embrace, in the enjoyment of its most perfect life, to permit them to fall into a temporary rebellion? Amazing work of faith in Jesus! wondrous power of Christian truth! glorious mystery of incarnate life and atoning death! The wondrous character of the important discoveries of science pales before the Christian mysteries of Divine Love.

X.

IS THE PRINCIPLE OF SELF-SACRIFICE ADAPTED TO THE DEEDS OF EVERY-DAY LIFE?

CHAPTER X.

IS THE PRINCIPLE OF SELF-SACRIFICE ADAPTED TO THE DEEDS OF EVERY-DAY LIFE?

MAN by the instincts of his nature and the necessities of his life requires to give his first attention to the external; and to the external he is conscious of a bias influencing him throughout the entire period of his earthly life. He requires to be well advanced in civilization ere he gives himself in earnest and attentive study to the internal of his being and life, and by so doing learns his true nature and requirements. Science should precede philosophy. The perception of this necessity leads to a correct and comprehensive knowledge of the principles of religion, and to the understanding of the conscious life of the spirit of man. The knowledge of the inner nature of man, and of the experience of the deepest principles of Christian life, is to be obtained by long observation and patient study of the spiritual in man, and of the varied manifestations of the Divine to the human in nature, providence, and grace.

Revelation began in figurative manifestations of Divine truth, and terminates in the enlightenment of the indwelling Spirit. The Church has had to pass through a series of varied experiences from the beginning of the work of redemption until now, and may be expected to pass through a varied process, during her earthly progress. And as with the Church, so with the individual believer. As man through the aid of physics and psychology learns the nature of the spiritual part of his being, and the personality of his life, he will give more attention to the principles of his inner religious experience than to the progress of ecclesiastical orders and forms of ritualism or of denominational distinctions.

The infancy of religious life was necessarily ritualistic and formal, then arose the ecclesiastical and doctrinal, and afterwards the intellectual and sectional. The Jewish Church followed this order of development, and in a similar manner the Christian is advancing. The decay of one condition or epoch precedes the advance of a higher and more spiritual and vital. The bane of religion is that the individual, the family, the social, and ecclesiastical life of man has been selfish. In no form of life on earth has selfishness appeared more baneful than in the ecclesiastical. No sooner does a religious man inbreathe the spirit of ecclesiasticism, than in the measure of such he sinks in his spirituality and godliness. The cure for all such evil must be the self-sacrificing of the Divine in the human.

The self-sacrifice of the Godhead is the glorious contrast of selfishness in man, and the self-sacrifice of the genuine disciples of Jesus in the imitation of their Lord is the needed power of the Church to raise her to the platform of apostolic times. The intelligent Christian, by the careful study of the Church's experience of almost nineteen centuries, will easily perceive that if the Church is to occupy the prominent position prophecy assigns to her in the latter days, and reign with the sovereign sway of apostolic times, she must give equal prominence to self-sacrifice now as she did then. The principle of self-sacrifice is the energy of the Church and the securing power of the loveliness of Christian life.

The spirit of self-sacrifice animating the man in power will prevent the abuses of the despotic spirit of selfish man, and secure the wielding of might only for beneficent ends. The spirit of self-sacrifice displaying itself in the rivalries of social life will restrain from all the abuses which are so lamentably common in the different departments of human intercourse, and secure the true results of the right spirit of emulation. The spirit of self-sacrifice manifesting itself in the sentient life of man will curb in him all undue indulgence of the appetites, all feeling of retaliation and desire for revenge, will secure temperance in all things. The spirit of self-sacrifice ruling in the different spheres and varied movements of human life would secure integrity in sovereigns, in cabinets, in governments, in politics, in executive functionaries, in commerce, merchandise, trade, in all the departments of professional life, in the entire intercourse of men. The spirit of self-sacrifice animating the religious life of the world would restrain men from self-righteousness, pietistic and ascetic abuses, ministerial officialism, clerical pomposity; from all vain and ostentations display in the religious profession, which offend good taste, provoke the sneer of intelligent discerners, perplex the minds of religious enquirers, and repel the wavering and doubting from making a profession of Christian life. The spirit of self-sacrifice regulating the lives of all who hold office in the public institutions of Christendom would secure the most blessed results. Were all in authority in prisons, in reformatories, in hospitals and all charitable institutions, in schools, colleges, universities, in the army, the navy, to live in the spirit of self-sacrifice, what changes for the better would be conspicuous among the nations!

Self-seeking instead of self-sacrificing being the underlying motive of religious effort with many who make great and persevering endeavours to be pious, leads rather to self-righteous deeds than to spiritual realization and growth in grace. Those who make such efforts are earnest in their devotions, they are persevering in their pious readings, they are diligent in their attendance on the observance of religious rites, ceremonies, and gatherings, that they may be the more pious and devout Christian examples to others; but they perceive not that in all this their efforts are "for" and terminate "on" self; they perceive not that all individual attendance on religious worship is serviceable only as far as it enables the worshipper to see into the spiritual nature, and to realize the elevating power of the self-sacrificing spirit of the Christian life; that all din, fuss, fervour, and gatherings for excitement for religious ends are a perversion of the first principle of Christian living.

While individuals endeavour to gain religious enthusiasm, climb into religious heights to be pious and devout for their own benefit, they attempt an impossibility, labour to effect a spiritual contradiction. Hence they may be loud in their praise of Jehovah, zealous in the worship of the Most High, and eager to realize the height of the Divine glory and sweets of blissful communion with God; but all to no purpose, for they are selfish, and being such they must be formal in their religion, contracted in their realization of the Divine, and barren in the fruits of spiritual life.

There is no labour on their part to acquire discernment, spiritual influence, and means wherewith they may meet the wants of the destitute, allure and guide the erring, minister to the sick, console the distressed, encourage the cast down, aid the struggling, reclaim the outcast, and to engage in such efforts not for their own spiritual profit, but out of love to humanity, devotion to Christ, and in imitation of Him. They have no desire like the Master, to be continually doing good in the several relations of life; and thus, not seeking their own, but forgetful of self, to reach the highest heights of spiritual life, and occupy the loftiest niches in the eternal temple of Fame, with the deepest and purest joy in their Christian living.

In the above statement it is not implied that to be pious, to attain to spiritual realization, and to grow in grace, are not in themselves godly aims, and worthy of earnest effort, devout aspiration, and persevering supplication; but it is asserted that those attainments cannot be possessed by fallen humanity in self-seeking, however strenuously pursued. "If any man come to Me, and hate not his father, and mother, and wife, and children, and brethren, and sisters, yea, and his own life also, he cannot be My disciple." Fallen man can attain to and advance in religious life only by self-sacrifice, and that consists not in one act or occasional deed, but in uninterrupted inbreathing and cherishing and exercising the spirit of self-sacrifice in all that is said and done.

But the spirit of self-sacrifice has a higher and more special function to discharge and mission to accomplish than that of regulating the intercourse of men in all the departments of social and religious life, so as to shun the evils which selfishness brings upon fallen humanity, and secure the advantages its beneficence cannot but confer. In its higher bearings, the spirit of self-sacrifice leads men to see how inducing a man to suffer that he may reclaim the wrong-doer to the paths of righteousness and peace secures the most beneficent results, as well as displays the noblest aspects of Christian character; such displays of self-sacrifice present religious influence to the eye of the world so as to arrest its attention and win its acknowledgment of the truth as it is in Jesus. Self-sacrifice necessarily involves momentary suffering, yet at the same time it awakes in the soul of the self-sacrificer the well-spring of the purest bliss and joy, which far outmeasures, and far more than compensates for the external suffering it imposes. Self-sacrifice on behalf of sinners leads to the conversion of sinners, and covers a multitude of sins. It thus secures a twofold benefit of highest character; a benefit to him who undergoes the self-sacrifice, and to him who is rightly influenced by it. If a cup of cold water given to a disciple in the name of a disciple is not to lose its reward, what must be the gain of saving a soul from death, of perceiving the beneficent results of the most benevolent deeds! The discernment of the glorious results in the world to come, of having been instrumental in saving a soul from death, must afford a pure, lasting, and satisfying joy.

The spirit of self-sacrifice is the noblest, most

beneficent, and self-rewarding, that can animate the finite or Infinite spirit. In itself and in its doings it is Divine. It may be cherished and acted on from the highest to the humblest of intellectual beings; it may pervade every thought, feeling, and action of every individual professor of Christianity; and were this to be the case, the millennial period of glory and bliss would be enjoyed all over the globe. It may be mistaken, and through mistake abused, but in itself it is infallible; no person breathing it into his every action would do wrong. Its trust is human dignity, glory, and bliss. To secure these it condescends to any depths, but never acts for the injury or wrong of any one. Meanness, grovelling servility, it knows nothing of, and can never stoop to; falsehood, pretence, and hypocrisy are abhorrent to its soul. This world of sin, degradation, and suffering is its true sphere of operation. Ambition is the atmosphere in which it most freely breathes.

What then is this spirit of self-sacrifice? and what does it do for them in whom it reigns, and for those in whose behalf it acts? It is the outbreathing of enlightened generous love, love of all that is real, right, true, and good in nature and in life. It weeps over sin and suffering, and while it strongly disapproves of the conduct of the perpetrator, it will bear with, nay, refuse to shun, his wrongs, that by its patient endurance it may win the wrong-doer out of his sinfulness, degradation, and woe, into dignified and happy life.

For its proper manifestation it requires no one to leave his position in society or his calling in life. It subjects to a momentary suffering, and it may be to temporary misunderstanding and misrepresentation and calumny, but it bursts open the well-spring of the purest bliss in the soul, and ultimately secures the brightest radiance of the enduring glory. Like mercy, it blesses him in whom it reigns, and all who are properly influenced by it.

Let but an enlightened teaching regarding the true spirit of self-sacrifice take possession of the pulpits of Christendom, and what a revolution would be wrought in the lives of all Church-going communities! A reformation greater than any of past times would ensue. There would then be no need of devising schemes for the garnishing of Christian life, with the view of retaining or drawing the youth of Christian communities into the Church, no need of gilding the services of the Church with the glittering tinsel of ritualistic manœuvring, to make them more attractive to the worldly minded. No, the Church as in the beginning would allure to her communion mankind in myriads. Devotion and zeal, while sufficient to bind the pure in heart, are not powerful enough to raise the fallen. This can be achieved through self-sacrifice alone.

And why should not the spirit of self-sacrifice animate every Christian breast, and fill every pulpit of Christendom? Is not such required by Christ, demanded by reason, and necessary to the believer's peace, and to the prosperity of the Church?

XI.

SELF-SACRIFICE THE ONLY PRINCIPLE THAT CAN RAISE THE FALLEN.

CHAPTER XI.

SELF-SACRIFICE THE ONLY PRINCIPLE THAT CAN RAISE THE FALLEN.

SELF, as we have seen, is degrading to man; whereas self-sacrifice is sublime, adapted to the nature and circumstances of man, and the sole condition of human elevation. Man thirsting for glory, by an indestructible law of his nature compelled to pant for distinction, may, through self-sacrifice, attain to the loftiest heights of being and life, and luxuriate in the pure consciousness of greatness. It is not too much to affirm that the chief cause of the Church's failure to raise the world to the sublime altitude of Christian faith is mainly attributable to her not realizing in herself the true grandeur and importance of the principle of self-sacrifice, and consequently not perceiving the true relation of ambition in connection with self-sacrifice to the work of grace.

As long as the Church contemplates man merely as a sinner, and the grace of self-sacrifice only as an evil incident to man's present circumstances, or as the endurance of penal suffering by his substitute designed to deliver men from the punishment of hell, she must be weak in her endeavours to elevate her own, and powerless to transform the life of the world. In so doing she keeps in view but a part of Christ's intention and work, she loses sight of the grandest portion of her calling, and neglects the chief element of human exaltation.

Why is it that the Church, while making extensive progress in heathen lands, is losing hold of the masses in Christian countries? This does not appear to be taking place from any superior power of infidelity, or from any indifference in the Church herself to her own possessions, but is traceable to her neglecting to direct the minds of her members to the glory of the Christian calling in its connection with the grandeur of self-sacrifice, in imitation of Christ, and enlightened devotion to the souls of men.

While Christ ever breathed the meek and lowly spirit, He always kept steadily in view the grandeur and glory of His calling. It was for the joy set before Him that He endured the cross, despising the shame; and His prayer was, "Father, glorify Thy Son," and "O Father, glorify Thou Me," and "The glory Thou hast given Me

I have given them." The Christian, in order to rise superior to the bewildering influence of the world, must ever keep in view "the mark for the prize of the high calling of God in Christ Jesus," "he must covet earnestly the better gifts," and steadfastly pursue the more excellent way; while he is never to forget that as a sinner he deserves banishment from the glory of God's power, and that by "the grace of God he is what he is;" as a believer in Christ, he is ever to remember that he has set before him "the crown of righteousness, which the righteous Judge shall give to all them that love His appearing," and that he has all the aids and facilities and encouragements which are fitted to induce him to follow Christ in the regeneration of the world. By co-operating with the Spirit of God in working out what He works in him to will and to do, he attains to the higher heights of the Divine life. It was thus that Paul was enabled to pursue his illustrious career. The Church has greatly erred in neglecting this aspect of her Divine calling, and this mighty power of her Christian work.

The greatness of the human spirit, its creation in the image of God, its capacity for union and communion with the essentially Divine, its capability of rebelling against God, of eternal conflict and anguish, of the consciousness of self-destruction, its possibility of regeneration into the Divine life, its possible conscious co-operation with the self-sacrificing Saviour, of fellowship with the Godhead in working out its own salvation, and aiding in the recovery of fellow immortal souls, are clear and unmistakable evidences of the innate greatness and possible glory of man's spirit, and ought to be matter not only of casual observation, but of the most careful study, especially by the members of the Christian Church.

The descent of the "Brightness of the Father's glory" into the arena of spiritual conflict, to accomplish the deliverance of man, the condescension of the great Self-sacrificer, in submitting Himself to misunderstanding, calumny, anguish, and death, in order to encounter and overcome the principalities of darkness, that He might set mankind the example of a glorious conquest, that He might exhibit to all intelligence the grandeur of the self-sacrifice of the Christian salvation, that He might afford to the Church the Divine principle and motive-power of her life and work, surely demands of every believer in Jesus the most careful attention and patient study, as well as the first place and chief homage of his heart.

Are the disciples of Christ wise in neglecting such an example? If the most illustrious of beings could heighten His underived glory by an acquired glory of character through the accomplishment of the most stupendous work of time or eternity, and if He came into this world of sin for the very purpose of undergoing self-sacrifice, that He might create the power and set the example of Christian life, surely it becomes those who are in this world of sin, His professed followers and fellow-workers, in working out what His Spirit works in them, to perceive that they are engaged in an undertaking that requires and is worthy of the profoundest self-denial and most arduous endeavours; that they are engaged in a work that will yet throw into obscurity the most dazzling splendour of one and all earth's greatest achievements, acquire glory that will envelop in darkness all the blandishments of time's greatest deeds of chivalry, statesmanship, philosophy, science, art, literature, poetry, philanthropy, wealth, and fame; and fire aspirations of the deepest, purest, most thrilling joy and delight possible to human consciousness.

The magnitude, grandeur, and blessed results of Christian life and work in this sinful world may in some measure be made apparent by a reference to Paul's injunction, "Work out what

God works in you to will and to do of His good pleasure." These words, perhaps more than any other we may take from the sacred volume, teach the magnitude and grandeur of the Christian calling on earth. They tell us that the end of the believer's work in time is to work out what the Spirit of God works in him to will and to do in the matter of self-sacrifice ; for this is that portion of the believer's co-operation which underlies his progressive advance in the Divine life ; and this is the work, above all others, in which God takes His supreme delight. Now, what can and what must be the magnitude, grandeur, and importance of that in which each person of the Blessed Trinity takes His supreme delight? Has the Godhead busied Itself in its inmost depths, laid its plan in the eternal council, created the universe of finite existence, sent the Brightness of its glory into the region of conflict to display its highest perfection in a deed of self-sacrifice, and to render it possible for man to co-operate with the Godhead in the manifestation of the power of self-sacrifice, that he may attain to the highest heights of glory and bliss, and is the believer in Jesus to fail to recognize his enviable opportunity?

To acquire wealth, to gain high position, to

value the honours, and seek the enjoyment of time, is far from being unworthy of the enlightened Christian. To be anxious about the virtue, the attainments, the positions, the success of children in life, is in no way unworthy of, but very becoming in, Christian parents; but to seek these in preference, nay, in neglect of the positions, honours, and enjoyments of the Divine, the illustrious attainments of the Christian calling, is unbecoming in the disciple of Jesus. To seek the things of this life for any other object than that of consecrating them in self-sacrifice to the cause of Christ, for the good of fellow-men, is unworthy of the imitator of Christ. The disciple of Jesus who lives after this manner reverses the Divine order of things; he prefers fellowship with the world in the sentient and imaginary, to fellowship with God in the illustrious and Divine of self-sacrifice; and thus he fails in opening up in his heart the purest well-springs of the water of life; he casts away the opportunity of living the most illustrious of lives, of accomplishing the noblest deeds, of acquiring the highest honours, and of enjoying the sweetest bliss; he makes himself a child, detains himself in the nursery, sports himself with toys, instead of advancing into the youth and manhood of Christian life.

To be in any way the instrument of separating an immortal spirit from its antagonism to the Divine, from its burden of guilt, its internal restlessness and conflict, from its vain endeavours to satisfy itself with the husks of the sentient and social; to be in any way the means of quickening the soul of man with the life of God, of imparting to it inner peace, enduring concord, unfettered freedom, pure satisfaction in the Divine, the consciousness of well-being, serenity, and bliss of life in the present and in the world to come, through self-sacrificing exertions, is to achieve a far nobler conquest than those of the great Napoleon, a more illustrious deed than that of Newton in deciphering the heavens, to confer a nobler boon than that of Columbus in bestowing a new world on his age; it is to snap asunder more galling fetters, and wrest from the most hideous of tyrants a freedom more illustrious than that which Bruce or Tell secured for their countrymen. Yes, it is to accomplish what is far more illustrious than would be achieved by the individual who should, if such could be found, do in his one life all that these great men have done in theirs. The glory of the true Christian life of self-sacrifice is brighter far than would be the glory of their illustrious deeds concentrated in one career.

The Church has had different work to accomplish in different periods or epochs of her history, and this was pointed out to her by her Divine Master. She had first to contend with her imperial persecutors, then with the corrupters of her simplicity, then with her ecclesiastical spoilers, then she had to indoctrinate with right conceptions of Christian truth, and to exemplify the power and beauty of faith in Jesus; and in the performance of such tasks she must never grow weary. But neither the Church nor the doctors of theology have as yet sufficiently seen that the great difficulty they have to contend with in indoctrinating minds with right views of Christian truth, and leading them into the realization of the power of faith, arises out of the fact that the world possesses not the Spirit of Christ, and that the Church of these days, in dealing with the world, has exhibited far too little of the self-sacrificing spirit of Christ; that in her work of seeking to enlighten the minds of men in Christian truth, and in her endeavour to induce men to imitate Jesus, she herself has forgotten "what manner of spirit she ought to be of;" she has too frequently lost sight of the fact that it is a possible thing to possess clear abstract views of Christian doctrine, and to exhibit a formal life of faith, while devoid of the real "Spirit of Christ," and thus come short of the fellowship of the inner life of self-sacrifice, and fail in her portion of the work of evangelizing the world. "If ye have not the Spirit of Christ, ye are none of His." "Hereby we know that He abideth in us, by the Spirit which He hath given us." Until the Church is baptized with a fuller measure of the self-sacrificing spirit of Christ, she will not, she cannot, attain to the perfection of the Divine life, appear in her glory, exert the influence on the world which is necessary to its turning to God.

The centralizing method of performing Christian work, adopted by the Church, has not a little interfered with the individual activity of disciples. Centralization, while necessary to the work of the Church in her aggressive advance on heathenism, in the spread of the gospel over all the earth, has been so allowed to occupy the attention of members, as to withdraw their minds from realizing their individual responsibilities in connection with personal effort. The one should be done, while the other should not be left undone. While the Church is to make every possible effort to advance in her aggressive operations on heathenism, till she shall comprehend all races of men among her people, and all lands within her pale, she is not to lose sight of her responsibility to those born in her midst, nor to let go her hold on those she has already won within her pale; and this she can only do by the self-sacrificing efforts of each and all of her disciples, embracing every opportunity, in the several relations of life, of exhibiting the beauty and power of Christian devotedness in self-sacrifice. This is especially incumbent on her, when the masses are drifting beyond her pale. Christians have been in danger of making an idol of the Church, instead of perceiving the beauty and divinity of self-sacrifice in the cause of Christ. The most ardent and persevering zeal, if in any degree breathing the spirit of selfishness in any of its numerous forms, must necessarily fail of promoting spiritual ends.

It is not implied that all in the Church can rise to the higher heights of self-sacrifice. There are some things in the Christian life which "all cannot receive" or attain to, and their acceptance should not be pressed on all. The same attainments should not be expected of all, no more than the same standard laid down for all. As there have been epochs in the development of the Church, so there will be diversity in the display of individual attainments, in all the periods and conditions of Christian life; and this variety contributes to beauty, as the rich display of colour in the floral kingdom.

XII.

THE ADAPTATION OF THE PRINCIPLE OF SELF-SACRIFICE TO THE NECESSITIES OF HUMAN WELL-BEING.

CHAPTER XII.

THE ADAPTATION OF THE PRINCIPLE OF SELF-SACRIFICE TO THE NECESSITIES OF HUMAN WELL-BEING.

CHRISTIANITY is equally adapted to all men, is equally offered to all men, is equally needed by all men, and is equally sufficient for all men; and requires to be equally embraced by all men to prove itself equally successful in all men. To secure the realization of this important fact in the experience of the rising generation, in the social ranks of the different communities, in the public life of the nations professing Christianity, every disciple must realize his individual responsibility and personal opportunity of shining in the true light of Christian self-sacrifice in this world of sin.

The Church's work in this and every age requires of her every member in his individual life and social connection, that he see and feel the necessity of making it his object, in all that he is and does, to let the power of Christ in

His self-sacrificing be seen in him. It is not to procure wealth, fame, power, and distinctions among the fashionable of the world that he is called of God, and placed in the Church of the Self-sacrificer in the midst of the sinful, but to display in the view of the world the power of Christ's life and death, to consecrate all that he is and all that God gives him to the cause of Jesus.

The history of the Church clearly proves that the gospel is the power of God unto salvation to every one that believeth. The preaching of the Apostles in their day, and of the Reformers in their time, was powerful to the conversion of sinners; but to understand why, it must be borne in mind that it was not the eloquence of the Apostles nor of the Reformers, but the exhibition of Christ in His self-sacrificing grace, by those who saw, felt, and delighted to exhibit the power of self-sacrifice in themselves, that was the power of God unto the salvation of others. Modern missions, reformatory and ragged schools, Bible-women, tract distribution, revival efforts, *are, have been, and will be successful* in the measure in which the spirit of self-sacrifice has been active in them. What the Church needs, is not the accommodation of the teaching of Christ to the tastes or likings of men, or that members of the body of Christ should conform to the customs and maxims of the world, but that each disciple should see and act on the conviction that his own spirituality and his influence on the world depend on the degree in which he lives in the display of the spirit of self-sacrifice.

The want then of the Church is that every member of her communion should realize his individual responsibility, seize his opportunities, recognize that the need of his time is that every believer in Jesus, from the highest to the humblest, keep steadily in view that he is called by Christ to shine in the light of the true, to live in the giving out of Christian influence, so that all who come into contact with him in the intercourse of daily life may feel the power of true Christianity. The demand of this age is, that each disciple live in the full consciousness that his influence on others, his own glory and joy, are conditional on his exhibiting the power of self-sacrifice in his individual sphere of life and personal calling in society; that for the performance of his peculiar portion of Christian work he is so to live that all coming into contact with him will be able to observe and admire the power of Christian principle, learn from him that Christian conviction can make man content, diligent, honest, generous, self-sacrificing, happy, in the humble, middle, or exalted circles of life. By so living he will do far more to commend the religion of Jesus to others, than by joining in the popular public efforts or party ends of much that is called Christian work. It is far easier in connection with such efforts to foster and display self, than in meek humility to manifest the spirit of self-sacrifice. It is an easy thing to be a self-conceited would-be great man in public life, it is a difficult thing to fill a prominent position in the meekness and gentleness of Christ. Hence the fruitless character of much so-called Christian work, that is sounded forth with popular applause. It is not so much the getting up of religious services, or the performance of religious deeds, as the engaging in every act of personal life in the self-sacrificing spirit of Christ, that is needed. Whenever this spirit animates individual life, these religious services and all that is necessary for the promotion of Christ's kingdom will be duly attended to.

The Christian is ever to keep in view that the gratification of sense, the acquisition of the things which minister to the honour and enjoyment of social life, are good in themselves, and when given by God, *i.e.*, obtained by honest industry, are to be possessed and used by the Christian. He is also to keep in mind that the legitimate power and enjoyment of these is far inferior to the possession and enjoyment of the Divine in Christ Jesus, and to prefer the things of sense and social life to the acquisition and manifestation of the things of God in Christ is unwise and undutiful. It is unwise inasmuch as it is not only to prefer the inferior to the superior, but by so doing to lose the true and proper enjoyment of both; for the Christian can really enjoy the things of sense and social life only in as far as he holds them in subordination, and lives for the things of the Divine life. It is undutiful to God, inasmuch as it is reversing the order of heaven; in so doing the Christian proves himself undutiful to himself, because he gives up the pure enjoyment of the Divine for the temporary, which perishes in the using. He is also undutiful to the world, because by so living the Christian neglects, nay, perverts, the only period and opportunity possible to him of so exhibiting Christian life as to exert its true influence of winning sinners to Christ. The Christian is to realize the true natural life of man by rising superior to the corrupt or selfish gratification of worldliness.

Let Christian parents imitate the Saviour, and

take their children into the arms of enlightened Christian affection, fold them in the bosom of Divine love, and draw out their hearts and associate their minds with whatever is gentle, pure, and true in Christian life, awake and foster in them the love of the Divine, impress them with the conviction that while secular education, attainments in wealth, comfort in life, standing in society, are all to be desired and followed after in their proper place, they can only be properly enjoyed as the Divine life is realized through grace reigning in the spirit. They are to be taught that heavenly-mindedness, or the consciousness of enlightened self-sacrificing devotedness to the glory of God in the good of men, is far higher in itself than worldliness, and necessary to the proper use and true enjoyment of the things of life. Such training will be the rearing them in the true atmosphere of Christian life. They may train them in the *finesse* of refinement, the highest code of morals, the most perfect creed of Christendom, and the most approved forms of devotionalism, breathe into their formal life the sweetest breath of piety; but if they leave them in selfishness, all will be vain.

Let the youth of all Christian lands be reared in the idea that vain foppery is unmanly and mean, that the display of egotism is childish, that the clinging to self-will and obstinancy is ruinous, that retaliation, cruelty, and revenge are devilish, that the acquisition of wealth, the possession of power, the attainments in rank, etc., are to be attended to only as means of progress in civilization, serviceable to the comfort and enjoyment of social life in as far as they are sought in subordination to the high ends of Christian life, nobility of spirit, godliness of heart, knowledge of the true, and fellowship with God in the self-sacrificing, and that these inner attainments are necessary to the pure enjoyment and honourable employment of the things of the outer life; that godliness is profitable to the life that now is, as well as to the life that is to come. Education in this form is the bringing of youth to breathe in the true atmosphere of manly and beneficent life.

Let the members of the Christian Church be taught that while they are not to neglect public, relative, personal duties in social life they are ever to bear in mind the necessity and importance of Christian truth, principle, and motive to the present and future life of man; that they have been brought by God into the Christian Church, to live for the true ends of human well-being, and while they are never to seek to force men into conviction, and lecture their associates into faith, never in any way to strive to coerce individuals into religious life, they are ever to keep in mind the condition of man in the world without God, the value of souls, the momentous importance of Christian life, the grandeur of self-sacrifice, and to strive to live in their respective positions in society, so as to draw men into the life of Jesus.

Let Christian youth, thirsting for nobler employments than those which mere sentient, social, or worldly life can afford to them, panting for glory worthy of the life God has given them, and the circumstances He has placed them in, have their attention properly directed to the illustrious work of the true Christian life, let them be taught to look for distinctions in the pursuit of "the mark for the prize of the high calling of God in Christ Jesus," let them, in the self-sacrificing spirit of their Lord, devote themselves to the performance of the illustrious deeds of self-sacrifice in the highest of all undertakings, let them learn the true nobility of fellowship with God in the prosecution of His glorious work, and they will not need to have Christian doctrine moulded to their tastes, or Christian life fashioned to their likings, to retain them within the pale of the Christian Church.

No, they will be strengthened with all strength in their inner man, and fortified against the bewitching sin of their individual constitution and calling in life, position in society, or relations in the family circle; they will, in the pure joy of an ever-abiding conviction that by the grace of God they are what they are in the calm serenity of a deep realization, know that true humility of spirit will not only sustain them under the difficulties, privations, and disappointments of their earthly condition, and make them in themselves more than conquerors, but also the honoured instruments of aiding others in their struggles after the Divine life. Instead of seeking to have Christian doctrine moulded to their tastes, or Christian life fashioned after their likings, their one aim will be to have their tastes brought into accordance with Christian truth, and their likings fashioned after the true type of Christian life.

And thus the Church will afresh be baptized with her youthful ardour, put on her beautiful garments, appear in her true attracting grace, and not in the spirit of pride or vaingclorying, selfish conceit or empty arrogance, but in the grace of true emulation, in the assimilation of the self-sacrificing spirit to Christ, believers will desire the noblest honours possible to finite existence, "covet earnestly the better gifts;" they will pursue the "more excellent way," which is the way of self-sacrifice, and not that of glorying in earthly attainments, or ecclesiastical distinctions, or pietistic or ascetic dreamings. And conscious of the quickening, sustaining, and grandeur of the indwelling strength of the Divine, they will enjoy the pure, the true, of sentient, social, and rational life, and the spiritual realizations of the grace of self-sacrifice.

The Church, in her zeal for the development of Christian doctrine, which she cannot with impunity neglect, has allowed the more talented of her sons to seek for distinctions in the regions of controversial debate and ecclesiastical dissensions, rather than in the higher walks of self-sacrifice, in keeping steadily before them the practical ends of the Church's mission in the world, *i.e.*, the seizure of the enviable opportunities and glorious means of enabling souls to realize the Divine, and consecrate themselves to the service of God. The Church has not kept sufficiently in view the adaptation of the gospel to man's nature and circumstances, especially to his native thirst for glory, and thus she has failed to keep before the minds of her more ardent converts the motive most fitted to hold them in their right path; and to this extent she has lost her hold on the more ambitious of her membership. (See Max Müller's account of the journey of the converted Brahmin to Christian lands, and intercourse with religious society in them.)

We cannot rid ourselves of the impression that it is in no small measure traceable to the Church's neglect to present before the minds of her youth the sublime motives, illustrious work, and glorious rewards of imitating Christ in His self-sacrifice for the regeneration of the world, and presenting instead of this such mistaken notions of Christian humility as she has done, that she is not now occupying the high position she ought to possess. She has encouraged her members to afflict their souls, to bow down their heads as a bulrush, spread sackcloth and ashes as an acceptable time unto the Lord, instead of teaching them to imitate Christ in His enlightened self-sacrifice. Does Christian life and worship really consist in pietistic acts of homage, in making a mere profession of membership, of adhering to mere forms of belief, living a formal moral life, devoting occasionally some material substance to Christian ends? Is it to be wondered that, in connection with such Christianity, the youth of the Church, instead of being drawn into the seizure of their glorious opportunities of living for Christ, are suffered to go into the world for distinctions, honours, enjoyments, and are thus allowed to conform to its customs in the nominal Church, and to fall away from Christ, and sink into the mire of pollution, and thus to grovel instead of rising to the sublime heights of the Christian calling? In her zeal to conform to the externals of religious life, she has lost sight of and allowed to fall into the background the true conceptions and inner power of clear visions of the lofty character of the work of co-operating with Christ through the indwelling Spirit in the self-sacrifice of the Christian calling.

It is patent to every observer, that as wealth, refinement, science, social industry, rational speculation, religious literature, Church efforts, are multiplying in Christian lands, crime, immorality, neglect of Christian ordinances, infidel boldness, are increasing in appalling force. And conferences about the state of religion, gatherings together for the consideration of public questions, loud cries for more religious zeal, discussions about the means and methods of checking immorality, lamentations over the increase of crimes, royal commissions for the improvement of penal discipline, delegate assemblies for the consideration of the most effectual methods of restraining vice and dealing with criminals, œcumenical, pan-Presbyterian, Anglican councils, attempts to patch up existing creeds, temperance societies, young men's Christian societies, and similar movements, expose the alarming state of Christian civilization, but are utterly helpless to effect a cure, or stem the current of vice, and in not a few cases make bad worse.

Wherein then lies the true power of Christianity, the power which has made her conspicuous in her zeal, glorious in her working, has carried her forward, and sustained her under all the opposition she has had to encounter? wherein lies the unperceived energy of the gospel of the Son of God to raise fallen man? Doubtless in the perception of the true dignity and ever-deepening bliss of self-sacrifice, and of what is inseparably connected with it, the inherent dignity and possible greatness of the human soul. The perception of Christianity being the greatest work of Godhead, the discernment of the glory and bliss of winning souls to Jesus, of raising fellow-immortals from sin and crime, by firing them with the love of the Divine, of enlightening their minds with the knowledge of the true, of guiding man's life in the noblest career of finite existence, seizing through self-sacrifice present opportunities of gaining immortal crowns; this is the true power of Christian life.

Let the unsatisfied restless heart, the ardent mind, the panting spirit of humanity, wasting its energies, enslaving its powers by giving itself to the false allurements of military enterprise, place-hunting, political scheming, wealth acquiring, pleasure-seeking, but obtain a glimpse of the true glory of man's life, taste a few drops of the pure water of life, and realize the rising of the Divine in the soul in connection with the deeds of self-sacrifice, and the believer will enter with ardour on the noble career of the Christian calling; he will escape the trammels of sense, the ensnaring allurements and captivating vanities of mammon, the fascinations of the frivolous, vain, and evanescent; he will realize freedom, dignity, and joy, live a life of unselfish usefulness, advance the cause of his Saviour God, exert a beneficent influence in his day and generation, and leave behind him a power for good to act ages after he has fallen asleep in Jesus.

Let but the Christian community realize that such a career is not only open to all, but that every disciple of Jesus is called of God to the performance of such deeds; that from the sovereign on the throne to "the beggar on the dunghill," all are invited by the great God of heaven and earth to be fellow-workers with Him in His glorious work of self-sacrificing grace. Let the aspiring spirits of humanity clearly perceive and deeply ponder the difficulties of the inner life, and the obstacles to the outer work of the Christian calling, and in humble dependence on sovereign grace, bravely encounter the arduous undertaking, and they will successfully overcome all the oppositions they have to encounter; in the true manliness of Christian fortitude they will buckle on their Christian armour, and go forth to the help of the Lord against the mighty, and they will be made more than conquerors through Him that loveth us.

XIII.

THE DOCTRINE OF CHRIST THE ONLY TEACHING ADAPTED TO THE NATURE AND CIRCUMSTANCES OF MAN.

CHAPTER XIII.

THE DOCTRINE OF CHRIST THE ONLY TEACHING ADAPTED TO THE NATURE AND CIRCUMSTANCES OF MAN.

WHY should the zeal of human ambition be wasted on the trifles of perishing vanities, and not devoted to the pursuit of the noble ends of life possible to man in the imitation of Jesus? Why should the Divine energies of the human spirit be squandered away on the acquisition of the mere sentient gratifications of an earthly life? Why should the noble opportunities of triumphing over the powers of evil in the accomplishment of that work in which the Son of God Himself has won His coveted glory, be thrown away on the acquisition of earth's vanities? Why should the sacred time of human life, given by God to man for the highest ends of self-sacrifice, be wasted in enslaving men to the bondage of self? Let every Christian realize the greatness of his Christian calling, "the high calling of God in Christ Jesus," and not be absorbed in vainglorying, but, glowing in the love of Christ, desire to be like Him, and strive to imitate Him in His self-sacrificing greatness, and he will live a life and exert an influence of the most illustrious and beneficent character possible to an immortal spirit created in the image of God, baptized and indwelt by the Holy Ghost.

Let the office-bearers of Christian lands perceive the dangers of officialism, its great liability to warp the spirit and pervert the powers of individual devotedness to the higher ends of life, and let them keep steadily before them the fact that, to the full extent of its influence on individual life, it blunts the edge of the keen perception of truth and privilege, and enervates the efforts of Christian beneficence. It is not by officialism that man can raise himself or aid his brother in escaping the bondage of self; no, but in breathing the Spirit and copying the example of Christ in His self-sacrificing devotedness. Let the sovereigns of Christian lands imitate the "Lord of Glory" (and such is their Christian privilege and imperative duty) in occasionally laying aside the insignia of royalty, clothe themselves with the spirit of meekess and humility, and while displaying the true grace of majesty in the spirit of self-sacrifice, visit the scenes of wretchedness, the abodes of crime, and while loathing the vice, love the humanity of the ungodly and vicious, and in the yearnings of Christian tenderness speak words of kindness with the accents of gentleness, forbearance, and mercy; and who can predict the results of such tenderness, condescension, and grace? Let the several members of the different royal households do likewise, and great will be their reward. Let the judge, who tries the criminal, lay aside his ermine, visit his justly condemned brother in the cell to which he has been removed from the scene of his conviction, speak to him in the meekness, kindness, brotherly love of self-sacrificing grace, and an immortal spirit may be gained to God, to humanity, and social well-being in devotion to Christian self-sacrifice, and on the expiration of his sentence he will return to honourable and honest life, an heir of God and a joint-heir with Christ. Let there be proper classification of prisoners. Let ministers of the crown, members of the aristocracy and legislature, magistrates, employers, parents, in their several spheres of influence, breathe and display the spirit of self-sacrifice, especially in connection with first offences, and great and numerous would be the reformations wrought in the social and religious life of mankind; few, if any, would there be of second offences. There would then be no dread of infidelity or communism, of revolution or of rebellion. Man will go astray (such is the inevitable result of his alienation from God), and the enviable privilege and glorious opportunity of the Christian in this world of sin is not to denounce the criminal, contenting himself with a mere formal life of morality, but to seize, in the spirit of self-sacrifice, the golden opportunities for reclaiming wrong-doers from the error of their ways.

Let the servants of Christ, the ministers of the gospel, from the highest to the humblest, lay aside the officialism of their ecclesiasticism, and in the meekness and gentleness of Christ, speaking in the spirit of self-sacrifice to their hearers of the glory of becoming like to Christ, and of imitating Him by aiding in the rescue of souls; let them act in the clear perception and deep realization of the power of Christian self-sacrifice, and what glorious things would be achieved in the different communities of the Christian Church! Let believers in Christ think aright of the glory, taste of the bliss, realize the responsibility of neglecting opportunities of winning souls to the Divine life, meditate on the reward of letting the light that is in them shine around, so as to draw even one soul to Jesus, and how influential for good would be the life of each disciple of Christ Jesus! The bliss of the inner joy would be pure in their consciousness of self-sacrifice for Christ in doing the highest possible good to immortal souls.

Let not these conceptions be thought utopian, or scorned as fanatical hallucinations, the disease of a wild enthusiasm run mad. Such sentiments will yet be universally entertained by the Christian Church. And such conceptions must not only be entertained but acted on by the disciples of Jesus, ere the world will be rescued from the powers of evil and the principalities of darkness, and the races of mankind converted to God. And such, if we mistake not the signs of the times, will be found necessary for the maintenance of social order, and the preservation of the harmony of the different relations of the political life of men.

Officialism, in one form or another, is necessary for the peace of the State and the harmony of the Church; but mere officialism will never prevent wrong, rescue from crime, arrest backsliding, or convert souls to Jesus. If officials would understand their true positions and legitimate function, and not turn their official standing to occasions of vanity and oppression, but employ their power for its right ends, they would live for the good of mankind. And if, after they had performed their day's duty, they would, as opportunities occur, exert themselves in heartfelt endeavours to raise the fallen from their habits of evil, by inspiring them with the love of right in the practice of self-sacrifice, they would not only be honourable members of civil society, but benefactors of their race in their imitation of Jesus. The mischief of prevailing notions is that it is only ministers and missionaries that are in self-sacrificing devotedness to seek and labour for the conversion of souls; and that all the officers of the State, the members of the several communities, and the professors of discipleship in Jesus have to do is to attend to the duties of their several callings and forms of religious worship. This is right in so far as it goes, if they do all that they do for the glory of God; but this is what they do not do, and hence the indifference to their opportunities in a sinful world of displaying the spirit of self-sacrifice in imitation of Christ. The more correct conception is that every believer in Jesus in his position should realize the privilege, obligation, and honour of seizing all the opportunities which God in His providence gives him of glorifying God in doing what he can for the promotion of the kingdom of Christ in the reclamation of others.

Then would all those who aim at being levellers in the Church and State cease their endeavours, and reverse their course of life and action. Differences in society and distinctions in life would seem to be in accordance with the nature of man, and necessary to the maintenance of order, as well as beneficial to the religious and social life of men. Not only would every act of his public calling, but likewise the spare hours of the disciple of Jesus be devoted to the sublime work of his high calling in God. This does not imply that he should neglect the exercise necessary for the preservation of health. Health, being the first of earthly blessings, and necessary to the proper discharge of social and religious duties, must not be sacrificed for any considerations; but living in the true spirit of self-sacrifice, a power over temptation would be gained, and a satisfaction in life acquired, which would go far to secure the best condition of health. If, however, instead of living for Christ in seeking the salvation of souls, Christians will conform to the maxims and customs of the world, they will not only deteriorate their own salvation, and lose precious opportunities of winning others, but will hinder the advancement of Christiantity in the world; or, as is too often the case, if they attempt to do the work of Christ in the spirit of Belial, whether in public or private life, they will only aid in the increase of infidelity and crime.

The pure atmosphere of Christian life is greatly needed by the Church and the world, for the welfare of man both in his civil and ecclesiastical life. As in the vegetable and animal kingdoms, so in the spiritual and social life of man. The vitality and development of the plant, the vigour and grace of the animal life, depend much on the atmosphere in which they are reared; in like manner, public opinion, popular motives, fashionable thought in Christian society, greatly affect the Divine life of the Church and the moral condition of the State. If the prevailing sentiments of the denomination or the religious ideas of the nation be worldly in their tone, ecclesiastical in their temper, pharisaic, pietistic, ascetic, and not Christ-like in their bearing, then will formalism, immorality, infidelity, increase.

But if the spirit of the Church, the sentiment of the nation, be after the mind of Christ in the spirit of His self-sacrificing, then will brotherly love, prosperity, and joy abound in all ranks of the community and conditions of life. The opportunities will be seized, and the energies of life devoted to the higher ends of man's existence; Christians will be ever ready to consecrate the fleeting moments of time, and to give their energies to the interests of spiritual life in self-sacrificing devotedness. Then would the several members of the community, perceiving and admiring the true nature and Divine necessities of man, be covetous of the "better gifts" of the "more excellent way," and consecrate their individual influence to the imitation of Christ in His self-sacrifice, and draw men into His holy life. Then would the life of the Church and the prosperity of the nation be not sickly and feeble, but lovely and vigorous. Such to a certain degree has been the experience of the past, and such will be the realization of the future.

The truth of the above will be at once apparent by a reference to the previous history of the world, and their bearing on the present condition of things will be also obvious to every careful student of the principles of man's religious and social life. The bearing of these principles on the religious and literary education of youth is far from being so carefully pondered, understood, and rigidly acted on as the state of society and the welfare of the race demand. It is well known that the study of the Bible has influenced the noblest minds and moulded the most generous hearts of modern times. The different States have found it necessary for the taking of evidence in their courts of justice to require an oath or appeal to the author of the Scriptures in evidence of the truthfulness of the testimony of the witness. Yet in the legislation of the day the framers of laws are desirous of excluding from the schools of the land the Book of books, the most influential and elevating instrument of the most important of all educations. This is carrying out the sectarianism of secularism with a high hand, but at the same time with the blindness of the worst of all forms of bigotry.

XIV.

SELF-SACRIFICE IS THE PRINCIPLE WHICH PERVADES UNIVERSAL BEING, AND MUST EMBRACE CHRISTIAN LIFE.

CHAPTER XIV.

SELF-SACRIFICE IS THE PRINCIPLE WHICH PERVADES UNIVERSAL BEING, AND MUST EMBRACE CHRISTIAN LIFE.

SELF-SACRIFICE, being the inmost principle and perfection of the Infinite essence, must pervade all creation and renewed life, in as far as these display the perfection and reality of the Divine. The doctrine of Jesus is that man, in order to well-being, must realize supreme love to God and fellow-love to man. Christ was the first to teach this doctrine, and exemplify it before men; and the progress of the Church, as well as the glory and bliss of the Christian, is conditioned on this principle of living. He also taught that the life of love is possible to man only as he breathes the spirit of self-sacrifice, and acts in belief of its truth. He likewise assured men that this life was in itself the most benignant and beneficent of lives possible to man, and that the only opportunity men will have of living this life is their brief period of existence in this world of sin; and that all who live this life with Him in time will reign with Him in eternity, in the loftiest and most glorious and blessed condition of existence.

The losing sight of this phase of the true Christian life was the greatest mistake into which the Church fell after the Apostles were taken from the earth, and from which error the Church has not yet recovered herself. Nor is it matter of wonder that in a distracted state of spiritual life she should, to escape from cruel persecutions, have entered into alliance with the worldly power of the State, and by so doing have yielded up the quickening grace of her life.

But in allying herself with such power she perceived not that she was exchanging the glory and bliss of self-sacrifice for the security and wealth of worldliness, and thereby parting with her true power, glory, and joy. Nor is it matter of surprise that in such an alliance the love of ease, pleasure, and distinction should have led the members of the Church to lose sight of the mark for the prize of the high calling of God, and to seek honour and gratification in ecclesiastical rank, crusades against the infidels, the fame of knights templars, ascetic mortifications, monastic seclusion, and nun chastity. The natural result of this perversion of Christ's principle of life in His Church could not but be that the different orders of ecclesiasticism that arose in the Church of the world should usurp the power and pervert the godliness of Christ's brotherhood, and by so doing prepare the way for the dark ages of superstition that followed.

The Church has had to retrace her steps of declension, and the reason why she has not returned to her former state of glory and power is that she has not yet clearly discerned the high place Christ has assigned to the self-sacrifice of brotherly love, and the necessity for its action, to the realization of the pure consciousness of fellowship with Him. It is not in ostentatious, false zeal, it is not in fuss about Church extension, it is not in angry controversy about purity of creeds and conduct, that the Church shines in the light that draws to Jesus, and makes her progress in the world, but in the calm beauty of enlightened self-sacrifice for the glory of God in the good of man. To the non-perception that this is the only way in which the Church can follow Jesus in the regeneration of the world is to be traced the chief cause of her failures in the great efforts and earnest endeavours of the leaders of the Reformation, etc., and that the Reformers should have been so blinded as not to perceive the lofty character and great importance of self-sacrifice in imitation of Christ is accounted for by the bitter controversies into which the Reformers fell about abstract notions, and the unfortunate rise of personal and sectarian rivalries. Christianity can advance only on her own principles.

The wisdom of Christ is conspicuous in the order established by Him in His Church. The influence of the world and the power of the remaining corruption of the life of the disciple must be counteracted by the opposite pressure of the glorious reward of following Christ in His self-sacrifice. It is to the want of due attention to the doctrine and order of Christ, and not to any defect in His principle and plan, that the apparent failure of Christianity in the world is to be traced. Man, in striving to attain the end of his existence, must have possessions, distinctions, religious consciousness; and Christ has seen this want of humanity, and made provision for its supply in the principle of self-sacrifice. The enjoyment to which He calls man's attention is pure and without alloy; the possessions which He enables man to acquire are internal and enduring, and far superior to any others possible to finite being; the distinctions which He holds out to man are lofty and elevating; the religious acquirements which He enables man to realize are such as meet his wants, energize his power, and fire his zeal. And thus Christ supplies man with all that is necessary and adequate to his permanent well-being.

The true atmosphere of self-sacrificing devotedness requires only to be brought afresh into the Church, the atmosphere in which Christ will be seen to be the grand Luminary of human life, the sphere of thought and desire in which the disciple can imitate Christ, and become like Him. When this atmosphere of spiritual breath is reproduced in the Church, the circumstances of individual life will fall into their proper place. In this atmosphere there will be no dallying with conscience in fulfilling the lusts of the flesh, in yielding to the corruption of fallen nature. Each individual will occupy his proper place, and be obedient to the heavenly vision. The cast and colouring of Christian society will not be such as allow the youth and simple-minded of the Church to follow the pursuit of vanities and worldly pleasure, but such as will draw them into the imitation of Christ.

The atmosphere of spirituality which Christ has given to His Church is the one which will inspire the thoughts and feelings of man to the pursuit of the proper objects and true ends of his existence. This is the only atmosphere in which man can fully and freely breathe in accordance with his nature, and find an object worthy of his life; to the accomplishment of which he can with heart and soul consecrate his powers, and in which he will find a motive adequate to all the conditions, contingencies, and hindrances to his fellowship with Jesus. If the true atmosphere of spiritual living which Christ has given to His Church be seen by His disciples to be the only one in which they can freely breathe and fully consecrate themselves to His service, they will the more readily give themselves with earnestness and diligence to the one end of their Christian calling. Let this atmosphere be so pure, that the disciples of Jesus shall as clearly perceive their opportunities, as fully value their privileges, and as diligently pursue the right end of their Christian calling as soldiers, lawyers, physicians, merchants, tradesmen, students, pursue the several ends of their calling, and they will consecrate themselves and their all to the one end of their existence.

Let but the spiritual and Divine of man's being and opportunities be as well understood and appreciated as the several objects of his sentient and social life, and then it will be seen and acknowledged that the deed of the "widow" in casting her mite into the treasury of the Lord is more illustrious in itself and more important in its results than all the hoardings of the millionaire; that the Bible-woman is greater in her walks of beneficence than the "belle" of fashion in all her flauntings in the gay and giddy circles of the world's dreamers; that the "teacher" in the Sabbath-school is nobler in himself, and more illustrious in his deeds, than the titled frequenter of the ring, the racecourse, the aristocratic gambler; that the promoter of ragged schools, the rescuer of "City arabs," the alleviators of human wretchedness in its numerous forms, are far more glorious and blessed in their deeds than the "leaders of armies," the amassers of fortunes, or the "popular winner of public applause" in any or all of its forms. The time is approaching when the life and the labours of a "John Howard," a "John Faulk," a "John Williams," will be seen and acknowledged to be far nobler and beneficent than the life of a "Leo the Tenth," a "Plato," or an "Alexander."

Let the heads of families, of communities, of nations, be but earnest in breathing the true spirit of self-sacrifice, and prudent in their endeavours to bring all whom they influence under the power of Christ's example, and how great would be the work accomplished, and how illustrious would be their fame! Such deeds, instead of being regarded as beneath their positions, or as interfering with the proper discharge of their daily functions, would be felt to be the adorning of their character, and ennobling of their virtuous lives in influencing for good all who came within the sphere of their actions. The want of the Church is that each professing Christian in his own sphere of life should breathe the pure spirit of self-sacrifice, and seize the passing opportunities which present themselves in connection with the discharge of the duties of his calling, and thus exert a wholesome and legitimate influence on all that move around them.

Christianity is adapted to all the circumstances and conditions of man's existence upon earth. Christianity for her promotion requires no man to leave his own position in society, or to occupy himself with anything foreign to his individual calling in life, but to keep to his own sphere, and in the proper discharge of his duties to exert the influence becoming his place among men. A mistaken zeal, leading professing Christians to intermeddle with things that lie beyond their sphere in life, works evil, and not good. It is in the proper discharge of the obligations of his own calling that the disciple of Jesus best serves Christ, the cause of humanity, and his own salvation.

Occasions will occur in which those occupying high positions may appear to step out of their usual walk in life to serve Christ, but it must be only in appearance. In such services they are only acting in harmony with their exalted rank, for they interfere with nothing belonging to others, or foreign to their condition in life. It is said of our illustrious Queen, when certain heathen visitants inquired of her the secret of England's greatness, that she led them not into the arsenals or dockyards of her navy, or to a review of her armies or fleets, but presented to them a copy of the Bible, and said, "This is the secret of England's greatness." In so doing she moved not out of her proper sphere, nor exercised an illegitimate influence, but took occasion to occupy what is doubtless the most sublime position, and performed the most illustrious deed of her reign. We have read of a leader of the House of Lords, while seeking health on the banks of the Nile, engaging in the labours of the "colporteur," that he might embrace the opportunity afforded to him of circulating the Scriptures in lands of darkness; and in such a deed he went not out of his proper sphere of action, but availed himself of a favourable opportunity of exerting a far more noble, though not a more legitimate, activity than what he performed in leading the British peers in their grave and responsible deliberations. It has been said of one of the Prime Ministers of England, that he taught in a Sabbath school; in so doing he went not out of his proper sphere, but set a noble example to others in taking part in what will make his name more illustrious, and secure a better reward than he could ever gain in his place in the House of Commons, or in presiding in the august Cabinet Council of the nation in its most solemn deliberations.

Let all who occupy prominent positions in society pursue a like course, and their deeds will be truly great in themselves, beneficent in their influence on others, and blessed in their reward. In the performance of such deeds, those who engage in them will only be doing what alike their common humanity and their common Christianity demand of them. The increase of the number of those who so live and act will go far to diminish the temptation in ecclesiastical circles to idolize those who engage in such deeds, as if they did something that was extraordinary in itself, and far out of the way of what Christian living required of them.

We have no desire to malign any of our fellow-men, or to bring a railing accusation against those who differ from us about what may be consistent in Christian profession; for we have received no such commission from the Master, nor been entrusted with such power of interference with the conscience or liberty of others; but we would in a friendly spirit earnestly inquire of those professing Christians who frequent theatres, ball-rooms, racecourses, betting saloons, midnight revelries, and such-like, to ponder well and carefully consider if such things be most conducive to man's physical and social well-being, if they feed the spiritual life of the soul, if they afford the best opportunities of imitating Christ in His self-sacrifice on behalf of man, or if they correspond with their Christian responsibilities, or can earn for them a glorious reward in the life to come. We would ask such persons whether, while souls are perishing in ignorance in heathen lands, while neglected outcasts at home are sinking in crime, while sick neglected children and indigent adults are dying of starvation in their own immediate neighbourhood, such frequentings be the most Christ-like methods of devoting their means and of consecrating their opportunities. Is it not their first duty and legitimate enjoyment to attend to the urgent claims of their common humanity? Let them reflect, and see if it would not be more noble, more beneficent, and more blessed to direct their attention to the wants of their fellow-men, and employ their means and opportunities in the rescue of immortal souls, by doing all in their power to draw them into the realizations and pure enjoyments of true Christian life. What if in the providence of God these helpless ones have been brought into their immediate neighbourhood that they might have the opportunity of cultivating the higher graces of the Christian life by attending to the necessities of the poor, the suffering, and fallen? The judgment day may disclose such a fact, and will the disclosure afford joy and comfort to those who for frivolous trifles neglected their golden opportunities?

It is said that Nero, while Rome was in flames, watched the progress of the fire from the top of a high tower, and amused himself in playing on the flute the drama of the destruction of Troy. Such conduct is rightly regarded with abhorrence, and viewed as indicative of the greatest profligacy. If true, it was certainly a manifestation of fearful wickedness and infatuated guilt. But is the infatuation and guilt less of those who, while possessed of the means and under the highest obligations to do all in their power to relieve the suffering, and save the souls of their fellow-men, neglect their opportunities, pervert their means, and waste their precious hours in frivolities, if not in madness? Is such conduct worthy of the Christian life, calculated to promote Christian ends, rescue the souls which Christ died to save, awake the consciousness of a pure and lasting satisfaction? Is it the self-sacrifice He has called men, in imitation of Himself, to make on behalf of their perishing brethren?

And we would ask those in the humble sphere of Christian society, who worry themselves in toiling with might and main to make gain, that they may vie with those in higher positions, and mimic them in their vain and frivolous deeds of empty, fashionable life, if it would not be far more satisfactory and nobler in them to seize their opportunities, consecrate their means, and employ themselves in the imitation of their Lord in His self-sacrificing devotion on behalf of the fallen and wretched. Surely Christ is more worthy of the imitation of professing Christians than the frivolous and vain. Were each class in society, and each individual in the

Christian Church, to live as becomes them, in exhibiting the true Christian life of self-sacrifice in the view of the world, and thus to display an enlightened zeal for the glory of God in the good of men, how much more consistent would their lives be, and how much more deep, pure, elevating, and enduring the happiness which they would enjoy, compared with what they derive from their imitations of the worldliness of fashionable life.

Jesus, in exhibiting in the view of the world the spirit and example of self-sacrifice, disclosed the Divine purpose and power of salvation, afforded a perfect illustration of Christian life, and in calling men to the performance of illustrious deeds displayed His deep insight into the principle of humanity, His full and comprehensive conceptions of what was necessary and adequate to move the spirit of man to the high and the holy. But while Christ has exhibited the perfection of His plan, His Church has failed to perceive what was clear in the view of her Lord, and by so doing has failed to accomplish her work in the world. In this the Church has followed in the path of the twelve, but will, like them, yet be raised to a higher state through the disappointments of struggle and self-sacrifice.

In losing sight of the true dignity of man, of the necessary requirements of human well-being, of the glorious rewards of the Christian calling, and substituting in their place escape from hell, sorrow for sin, and the mortification of asceticism, theologians have wrought unspeakable mischief in the Church, and done great wrong to the world. Man as instructed by Christ is not to endeavour to work himself up to live for God, that he may escape hell and gain heaven; but he is, by faith in the gospel, to realize an enlightened love to God, for what He is in Himself, and for what He is to man, and in the perception of the true dignity of humanity he is to strive to live worthy of his nature, means, and opportunities, in the conviction that in no other sphere can he engage in such illustrious deeds.

The love of glory, the desire for distinction, the thirst for enjoyment, being innate in man, nothing that robs him of, or fails to secure such to him can long engage his affections, occupy his thoughts, or concentrate his energies. To seek heaven in order to escape hell, to serve God for the benefit of self, to devote the things of time to merit the things of eternity, is to mistake the very nature of the Christian salvation, and to stumble on the threshold of a noble career. To pursue successfully his noble course, the disciple of Jesus must perceive that as his Lord, "for the joy that was set before Him," entered on His self-sacrifice, so must he imitate Jesus in rejoicing and being "exceeding glad" when reviled and persecuted falsely, knowing that in himself he is blessed, and that great is his reward. By inspiring men with the love of God, and by the prospect of glory alluring them to the imitation of His own sublime life and heroic deeds, Christ supplies man with the principles and motives which alone are adequate to a successful encounter with and triumph over the evils of his present state, and which are necessary to enable him to turn these evils to the occasion of the highest possible advantage for the discipline of his own life and the benefit of others.

The disciple of Jesus engaging in acts of self-sacrifice from love to God and his fellow-man, perfecting his own salvation as he does what he can, in accordance with his position and circumstances in life, to promote the salvation of others, lives the most glorious of all possible lives on earth, and performs his portion of the most glorious work of time. And to aid and encourage him to persevere, he must keep in remembrance that the glory which Christ now enjoys as the great Redeemer of men, and will enjoy throughout the everlasting ages, is not the glory which belongs to Him as the "Brightness of His Father's glory," but that which He has won by His life and death of self-sacrifice on earth.

The life devoted to the cause of Christ is not only in itself the most glorious, but is also the most blessed a man can live on earth. No delusion regarding Christianity is greater than that which contemplates the Christian consciousness as one of narrow, morose, sad realization, although the delusion is easily accounted for. The Christian's is a far happier life than the man of the world's. Happiness will never disclose her loveliest beauties or bestow her choicest favours on the frivolous pleasure-seeker, whose joys are like the "cracklings of the thorns under the pot." The happiness of the Christian consists in a conscious union and communion with God, in an exchange of heart, in the giving of a pure affection to the reception of the sweetest inflowings of the Divine, in the consciousness of being upheld and guided by infallible power and unerring wisdom, in the consciousness of living for the highest possible end of life, in the consciousness of employing the best and most suitable means for the promotion of the most glorious and blessed work, in the consciousness of living in accordance with the will of the Father, the end for which the Son became incarnate, suffered, and died.

And not the least part of the benignity and wisdom of Christ's plan is that every one of His disciples, however apparently humble and insignificant, can take part with Him in the regeneration of the world, and share with Him in the blessed and glorious rewards of His self-sacrifice. Whatever may be the position of the disciple in his particular sphere of action in life, there is work for him to do. And so complete is Christ's plan of operation, that no disciple following Him requires to leave his position in society, or to alter his circumstances in the social scale of life. All that is required of him is to live by faith, in the contemplation and reception of the Divine, so as to be able to consecrate himself and his all, that he may shine in the beauty of Christian life, in the discharge of the several duties of his respective calling. So living he will be able to win souls to Christ, not indeed by ostentation, but by the silent beauty of true Christian vitality, in which he so gently moves as not to let his left hand know what his right hand doeth.

The good deeds of the genuine disciple of Christ are not the fruit, flowers, leaves, twigs, and stems of artificial waxwork, but the genuine stems, twigs, foliage, blossoms, fruit of a vigorous Christian life.

The point at issue between the believer and the unbeliever in Christ is within the compass of a nutshell, and of easy test. The evidence of the wisdom of the one and the folly of the other is not far to seek, but is near at hand, and can at any moment be adduced. The past experience of the world proves most clearly that all the efforts made to raise man by secular education, rational development, scientific discovery, philosophical speculation, political science, moral reformation, æsthetic refinement, ascetic fastings, social elevations, however earnestly originated and diligently persevered in, have invariably failed, and can never succeed. They can never meet the deep capabilities of man's nature, occupy the void of his immortal soul, lift from his conscience the load of guilt, allay his inner distress, harmonize the principles, relations, and operations of his life with themselves, with God, and with the end of his existence, raise his aspirations to the genuine standard of his well-being, and supply him with the true motive power and invigorating nutriment of the Divine life in his soul. But Christianity is possessed of this power and bread of life; this is that which distinguishes her from all mere human systems, and in the application of her motive power to the soul of man she does all that is necessary for his true elevation. It is her glory and boast, that she will raise men only in the measure in which they drink in her pure spirit, yield their minds up to her unadulterated truth, and live by her motive principle and power of life. It is in this manner and degree of raising men that Christianity has never failed. The past and present success in elevating and blessing the life of man proves and clearly proves that whensover she has been understood and persistently acted upon, she can and will do all that is needed for the present and future well-being of the entire race of mankind.

In fine, the principle of self-sacrifice pervades the entire of universal being in its operations and life, the heavens shine in the splendour of their celestial glory, not for themselves, but for the being created in the image Divine. The earth brings forth in the luxuriance of her rich abundance, not for herself, but for man, placed over her by the act and authority of his Creator; vegetation arrays herself in her beautiful robes, not for herself, but to gladden the heart of man. The animal in all his rich variety exists not for himself, but for his owner and lord. And man lives not for himself, but for his fellow and his God. He fills and performs the duties of his many offices, not for himself, but for the benefit of general society; if he fills such for himself, he only degrades his life and injures his fellowmen; but if he discharges the duties of his rank for the good of others, he by so doing brings honour on himself, and benefits others. The true student cultivates his intellectual powers, not so much for the benefit he expects to derive in his after-position in society, as from his love of mental cultivation and the dignity it secures. The child of God who understands his privilege and responsibility lives not unto himself, but unto Him that loved him and gave Himself for him, that He might redeem him unto Himself, and purify him from all iniquity. Paul, the self-sacrificing apostle of Jesus Christ, was a far more illustrious and happy man than selfish Saul in the persecuting spirit of his mission to Damascus. In short, nature through all her works proclaims aloud that the Creator delights in self-sacrifice.

XV.

SUMMATION.

CHAPTER XV.

SUMMATION.

IN Christ's declaration that He came not to be ministered to, but to minister, and to give His life a ransom for many, we have a statement which discloses the essential nature of Christianity, and the necessity of the infinitude of Christ. The conception of not being ministered to, but of ministering by conditioning His manifestations to the production and reclaiming the highest life to the purest enjoyments of the loftiest fellowship is the most profound, comprehensive, and sublime of Divine ideas, an idea only possible to the consciousness of Infinite fulness, to the consciousness which divides the Infinite from the finite life.

The finite acquires greatness in being ministered unto. It has nothing of its own, but is dependent in all that it is, achieves, and attains to. The Infinite displays greatness in ministering. By producing and maintaining the finite in existence, by superintending the development, or regulating the evolutions of progressive existence, the Infinite manifests His fulness. In yielding to the bitter exasperations of enmity for the re-claim of rebel life from abnormal selfishness to filial devotedness in the annihilation of the rebel spirit, through voluntary self-sacrifice, the Conditioned displayed a purpose of will which was possible only to Him who was conscious of being the outcome of the Absolute.

Ambition, or the eagerness to shine in the effusions or the supposed attainments of life, seems to be the deep-seated principle of personality, and is apparent in the manifestations of the Infinite and in the movements of all finite existence.

The Infinite shines in what He emits, through the conditioning of Himself in evolution and self-sacrifice. For what is creation in all its vast, varied, enduring forms, but God manifesting Himself by coming under the forms of limitation, as He conditions Himself to the accomplishment of the ends of His love? And what is the self-sacrifice of the Godhead, but the Father giving the Son of His love to the conditions of the reclamation of rebel spirits, or the conditioned of the Divine yielding Himself up to the wrath of the rebellious? God has an end in view in all the manifestations which He gives of Himself, and this end is worthy of His unerring wisdom. It is not an end of mere display or of vain ostentation, no, nor of insufficient revelation, but of "fulness of impartation." The Divine heart realizes its fullest delight in the creation and redemption of the objects of its tenderest affection, by means of evolution and self-sacrifice. The creation of the finite leads to the possibility of evil, and the overthrow of evil necessitates the operations of self-sacrifice.

The human shines in what man receives, appropriates, and displays of the Divine, and only of the Divine, in the normal operations of his life. There is nothing in man of a self-creative nature or of a self-sufficing character. Man attains to the perfections of his being only in as far as he receives, appropriates, and manifests the Divine in accordance with the law of his life. In his normal actions he realizes the Divine capabilities of his nature and the grand possibilities of his life. If in anything or in the least degree he deviates from the law of his life, or the normal conditions of his well-being, he displays self, and falls from his true eminence.

The worldling or selfish man shines in his worldliness by seizing, through exaction, usurpation, or oppression, the property, and by domineering over the lives of others. In all the aims and efforts of his life the worldling desires and labours for his own selfish ends. He cherishes the thoughts of accumulation, and acts on the principles of exaction for his own individual benefit, and for the advantage of his dependants. The worldling has no conception of accomplishing the ends of life by giving himself in self-sacrifice for the advantage of others, and much less for his enemies. If at any time, in peculiar circumstances, he should feel constrained to appear in the formal of self-sacrificing deeds, it is only for the accomplishment of his own ends. In his life of selfishness, without being conscious of it, the worldling, in gratifying his own vanity, and securing the physical and social benefits of his family, ignores his higher nature, shuts himself out from the purest enjoyments, the noblest honours, and most enduring rewards possible to man, and at the same time injures, if he does not finally ruin, all whom he influences.

The Christian shines in what he receives, appropriates, and displays by means of self-sacrifice. Fallen man can be a Christian and can make progress in Christian life only in the measure of his self-sacrifice. It is only through self-sacrifice that the sinner enters upon the life and realization of regeneration, and it is through self-sacrifice that the believer in Jesus advances in sanctification, or builds himself up in holiness. It is only through self-sacrifice that the disciple lives for Christ in this sinful world. The bias of the carnal mind, or the efforts of the old man still remaining within him, the example, prejudice, and influence of society around him, all tend to induce him to gratify self. And thus the believer must ever be on his guard, and bear in mind that in the exact measure in which he lives in self-sacrificing devotedness for Christ, he lives, realizes, and becomes glorious in the Divine.

Christ's mission for the sole purpose of ministering necessitates not only the consciousness of absolute fulness, but likewise His descent from the infinite into the finite of life. A mere finite being, in order to the perfection of his life, must be ministered unto. But a being that comes under conditions for the sole purpose of ministering to others, must possess the consciousness of infinite and eternal fulness. And the Being that comes under the most humiliating condition, that by self-sacrifice He may allure His enemies to the enjoyments of the highest life, must not only possess the consciousness of boundless fulness and immaculate purity, but be actuated by the tenderest yearnings of Divine love. And thus it is that Christ's coming to minister to the deepest necessities of the fallen in offering Himself on their behalf, opens to our vision the inmost recesses of the absolute. Christ's display of self-sacrifice not only discloses the deepest depths of the Divine, but proves to universal intelligence that there is no other principle by which the fallen can rise to the enjoyment of purest fellowship with the "Father of all."

If the Son of the Father condescended to such conditionings of limitation, humiliation, and suffering, that He might win glory and open the deepest well-springs of bliss, then must it be evident that regenerated life among the indigent and suffering is the most enviable state of temporal existence the divinely quickened can desire. In other words, the being put into possession of the means, and afforded the opportunities of exerting themselves in self-sacrifice on behalf of the unworthy, is the true sphere of manifesting the Christian spirit, in living the Divine life, and the only period of displaying the genuine Christian zeal of self-sacrifice.

As the sun is set in the heavens to shine in the light of day, so Christians are made sons of God, gifted with the life and light of truth, and continued in this world of sin, that they may exercise the powers and manifest the necessary properties of the Divine life, in ministering to the necessities of the indigent and suffering. They are not gifted with the qualities and functions of the Divine life to lie latent in their souls, but to enable them to acquire greatness in manifesting the Divine that is in them, as they minister to the necessities of fallen man. In the consciousness of his Divine ministrations to the needy, the Christian man is great in action, lofty in character, noble in enjoyment, a steward of the manifold grace of God. Christians are made sons of God, not to employ for themselves or their families the graces bestowed on them in seeking selfish ends. They are, whether they eat, or drink, or whatsoever they do, to do all to the glory of God. They are to bear one another's burdens; to suffer the loss of all things. Not to forsake Christ, as Demas, for filthy lucre. For if they do so, then their riches will be corrupted, their garments moth-eaten, their gold and silver cankered, the rust of which will eat their flesh, as it were fire.

And thus it was that the Apostles, while gifted with the power of working miracles on behalf of others, and of raising the dead, had themselves both to hunger and thirst, were naked and buffeted, had no certain dwelling-place. And amid such trials they so rejoiced in their lot, that they took joyfully the spoiling of their goods, knowing in themselves that they had in heaven a better inheritance.

They knew why it was, and for what end they were gifted with the powers and properties of the Divine life, and could not allow themselves to remain among fellow-immortals in a world of sin without exerting themselves to the utmost of their power to allure sinners to God. They saw their opportunities, they felt their responsibilities, they coveted the joys, honours, rewards of self-sacrifice in imitation of Christ. They sought to be in the world as Christ was in it, that they might be made comformable to Him in His death, so as to appear with Him in His glory.

The watchword of the Christian is not truth, law, humanity, but God, the Redeemer of men to truth, law, humanity. God, by the disciple of Jesus, is not looked to as the Avenger; truth is not regarded as an idle speculation or worship; law as a restraint; humanity as the end of man's life; the world as the arena of self-seeking; time as the chance of making gain. But God is looked to by him as the loving Father, redeeming man in His own Son from selfishness to self-sacrificing devotedness. Truth is regarded as the light of love, guiding the inquiring spirit into the discernment of the principles, laws, and realizations of the highest life. Law is held to be the safeguard of the loyal, and devout humanity is loved as the true temple of God. The world is held to be the suitable sphere of Christian self-sacrifice, and time as the precious moment of being spent in the imitation of Christ in His devotion to the glory of God in the good of men.

Faith in God through the Lord Jesus Christ so quickens the spirit of the believer in raising it in love to God, and in drawing it forth in love to man, as to enable the Christian to avoid the extremes of indifference, and intolerance enlightens his mind in the harmony of life, and gives him to apprehend all that pertains to human blessedness in its fullest extent.

And thus idolatry, speculation, asceticism, inhumanity, tyranny, licentiousness, sloth, ease, luxuriousness, and vanity are shunned. Man in the faith of the gospel adores with ardour and delight, worships in truth and righteousness, realizes in the beauty of holiness, honours humanity as the supreme of finite existence, glorious as indwelt by God, lives for its emancipation from sin, seizes his opportunities of relieving the suffering, aiding the struggling, encouraging the timid, invigorating the weak, and rejoices in the honour and comforts of life in all its normal realizations.

Man thus receives the Divine life that he may realize its fullest perfection in ministering to the suffering of earth in the tender compassion of self-sacrifice, to the cause of Jesus. And like the Master, the disciple finds his joy not in breaking the bruised reed, nor in quenching the smoking flax, but in being alive to all the interests of man, in exemplifying the true principles, of raising the civilization of fallen humanity to its highest conceivable degree, in taking children in his arms and blessing them, in being present at the marriage feast, in succouring the wretched, and in raising the fallen.

To conquer and subdue, not by the brute force of destruction, the prowess of domineering pride, enslaving the mind by binding its conceptions to the forms of finite thought, but by yielding to emnity in order to change it into love, that it might unite itself to all that is true, elevating, and Divine, to enable it to realize the highest life, the purest enjoyments, in consecrating itself to universal well-being, in the discharge of the duties of the Christian's noble calling, embodies a conception of life in this world which is impossible to the selfishness of fallen humanity, and discloses a conception which could have come only from the self-sacrificing God.

Every peculiar doctrine of Christianity is in itself a clear proof of its supernatural character, and a powerful argument for the Divine origin of the gospel of the Son of God. And the gathering together into such a form all these sayings of Christ would render an eminent service to the Church.

XVI.

CONCLUSION.

CHAPTER XVI.

CONCLUSION.

ERE closing these pages, we would earnestly address a few words of counsel to our fellow-men, and especially to the youth of our Christian country. Fellow-immortals, if you have perused the previous pages with even a slight attention, it must be apparent to you that the all-important change in human life by which man passes from the service of self to the service of God, from sin, degradation, and misery, to holiness, dignity, and bliss, is produced in man by the agency of the Holy Ghost, the Eternal Spirit of the loving God. It must also be apparent to you that the Spirit produces this change, not in opposition to, or irrespective of, but by means of and in harmony with individual co-operation with Him. It is therefore your incumbent duty and enduring interest to examine into the evidence, and read the truth as it is in Jesus; and as you do this, to wait on the ordinances of Christ's appointment, to ask from

God the gift of His Spirit, that He may take the things that are Christ's, and show them unto you. And to do this in the conviction, that if a selfish parent, possessed of an abundance of food, would not give a stone to a hungry child entreating for bread, much less will your heavenly Father suffer you to ask the Spirit in vain. And to prevent any hindrance to securing an answer to your prayers, be careful not to resist the Spirit of God awakening the risings of the Divine life in your soul, and be very attentive in working out what the Spirit of God works in you both to will and to do of God's good pleasure.

You must assiduously guard against the one great hindrance to co-operation with the Spirit of God. This hindrance consists in your selfishness, which manifests itself in your disinclination to undergo this change, and your false conceptions of the nature and results of the change. You imagine, if you become the subject of this change, you will have to forego the desirable if not necessary pleasures, sports, and agreeable society of life, and give yourself up to sadness, melancholy, and seclusion; in other words, make great self-denial in foregoing the benefits of your sentient, social, and rational life. Permit me to correct this mistake by assuring you that instead of foregoing the benefits of your sentient, social, and rational life by this change, you will only secure them in a much higher, purer, and more lasting measure. It is only the sacrifice of self that you are called to make, *i.e.*, to part with what is corrupt in you, and what confines you in your spiritual disease. It is in partaking of the medicine of a Divine cure that you can enjoy better health of body, truer health of spirit, mind, life, and fellowship with your Father in heaven. You have only to part with whatever in you rises up against God, and your own true and permanent well-being, whatever in you interferes with the real operations and enduring benefits of your sentient, social, rational, and spiritual life.

The sacrifice which you make in parting with what you do give up is worthy of you as the subject of this change; it is the slaying the deceitful, the foregoing the baneful pleasures, the parting with the false and misguiding notions, the injurious practices and corrupting society of the world, while you receive in their stead the quickening of the Divine, the light of the True, which are necessary and adequate in enabling you to realize the real and enduring pleasures, truthful conceptions, elevating recreations, illustrious and ennobling society of the true, good, immortal, and Divine. In short, you receive from God, in fellowship with His Christ, all that is necessary to meet, fill, enlarge, and invigorate the capacities, powers, and aspirations of your souls, occupy aright the faculties and functions of your mind, secure your true peace and comfort in enabling you to live for the individual, family, and social well-being of mankind, and for the glory of God, by shining in the beautiful and blissful character of true Christian life.

Christianity asks no man to forego anything but what stands in the way of his highest good, and the real and permanent benefit of each and all the members of the human race. And if, in consequence of the selfishness of the world, she call upon any of her disciples in particular circumstances to forego any external advantage for a brief period, she in return secures for him a far more valuable and lasting benefit. And just as Christianity advances in the world, or to put this in another form, as the men of the world are raised by Christ to the higher life that is in Him, will all such demands diminish and become less known. What you part with in becoming a Christian is the vitiating for the pure, the false for the true, the wrong for the right, the tormenting for the enjoyable, the degrading for the honouring, the obscure for the illustrious, the carnal for the Christian; and you have only to reflect on this change in the light of its humanizing influence to perceive its reasonableness in a sinful world. It is only in the heroic sublimity of self-sacrifice that you can enjoy life in accomplishing the all-satisfying, grand, and glorious end of your existence.

Think of the importance of that, for the further accomplishment of which a man of Paul's intelligence and experience would be willing to expose himself to fierce persecution, and for a season forego the glory and joy of heaven, the anticipation of which entranced his soul; nay, think of the importance of the salvation, for the effecting of which the Logos of the Godhead descended to the deepest depths of humiliation and suffering, that He might win the glory and joy of accomplishing so great a work. To engage in such an enterprise on earth, and by so doing prepare more effectually for the fuller fellowship of its honour and bliss in heaven, is doubtless infinitely to be preferred to the places, the power, the wealth, the pleasures, the fame, the empire of earth in the brief period of a mortal life.

Is it then unreasonable for Christianity to call upon you to forego the brief, unsatisfying, hurtful pleasures which one who spoke from an enlarged experience, as well as from inspired conviction, compared to the crackling of the thorns under the pot, and in their stead to accept the recreations and joys which satisfy and elevate in every possible manner and endless degree? or is it unreasonable in you to give up your deceitful pleasures for enriching joys, your false notions for true conceptions, your degrading sports for ennobling exercise, your ruinous society for illustrious companions? Is it really unreasonable in you to yield up your capacities, powers, and aspirations of soul to Divine influence, eternal truth, glorious employment? Is it, indeed, unreasonable in you to become the instruments, the agents, the co-operators with God's own Son in the accomplishment of the noblest undertaking of time, by acquiring in yourselves, and by conferring upon your fellow-immortals the divinest gifts God Himself has to bestow, or to aid in carrying forward to its consummation the greatest and most illustrious design of the Eternal Council of the Godhead?

Brethren, is it unreasonable in us to invite, or is it insulting to your intelligence to plead with you that we may induce you to give your most serious attention to the consideration of this most momentous theme, or urge upon you to embrace that truth which enables you to seize the brief and only opportunity that will be given to you to engage in the true, heroic, and sublime of self-sacrifice, and of taking the part assigned to you by Infinite wisdom and benevolence in the undertaking whereby you become fellow-workers with God, and enter into the realization of the most pure and lasting enjoyments, and are entrusted with your part in the performance of the most glorious and beneficent of deeds?

Suffer not your minds to be perplexed, nor your hearts to be hardened from embracing these views of truth and realizations of life, by any of the conflicts which in these days arise between theologians and scientific *savans*. Keep steadily in view that, as the medicine of cure in allying itself with the powers of vitality in the physical frame of man has much to encounter and overcome in the operation of disease in the body, so must the Christianity, which is the restorative power of man's spiritual life, in entering into conflict with the disordered operations of a sinful nature and worldly life, have to encounter and overcome powers, prejudices, and sinful biases, both in scientific, speculative, and theological creeds. And as in her restorative operations Christianity discloses the unity and harmony of all real principles, powers, laws, and operations of being and life, so will it be seen that the truths of Christianity and science are one and harmonious. This fact is becoming apparent in astronomy, geology, chemistry, physiology, and will be so in development and evolution. This will be made plain just as the knowledge of man advances and enlarges.

And we would ask of the well-meaning, though often misguided professors of Christianity, if they are wise in holding up to the view of noble-minded inquirers after truth, and to the young, who are earnestly groping their way to the embrace of the Divine, a caricature of spiritual-mindedness, instead of the genuine image of the life of Jesus. These youthful truth-seekers require to have presented to their gaze as genuine an illustration of the spirit, mind, and life of the Great Master as it is possible for the disciples to exhibit. It is incumbent on you to display before them the cheerful, radiant countenance, the calm, enlightened mind, the noble, forgiving spirit, the self-sacrificing devotedness which Christ imparts to

His genuine disciples, which enables them to occupy any position, mingle with any class of society, take part in any and every enterprise which has for its object the good of their fellow-men, and restrains them from all that is doubtful or liable to misconception.

It becomes you to exhibit to these truth-seekers the fact that time spent in public worship, and seasons devoted to devotional acts, are beneficial to man only in as far as they are instrumental in feeding the soul with the Bread of Life, enlightening the mind in the knowledge of the true, and fortifying the conscience in the hours of temptation; that it is faith and fellowship with God that is true godliness, and that by whomsoever and wheresoever these are fostered in the heart, they will produce the genuine fruit of righteousness in the life, and will do so in accordance with the constitution and circumstances of the individual believer. It is incumbent on you to show these youthful truth-seekers that the Christian, in the consciousness of the pure and deep welling up of joy in his spirit, in the calm, satisfying peace of his mind, the greatness and grandeur of the object of his life, can easily forego the worthless and baneful excitements, the empty and selfish vanities which the restless spirits, the troubled minds, the burdened conscience, and fatigued life of the ungodly urge him to rush into in the hope of finding his chief good, but instead of which he only realizes further disappointments.

You must be careful to bear in mind the proneness of the partially enlightened disciple to desire, seek, and endeavour to get the principles of the Master to comply with his inclination and circumstances, instead of realizing his obligations to truth, and the necessity of continually striving to bring his heart, mind, and life into conformity with the requirements of Jesus. You are also to bear in mind, and strive against, the readiness of disciples to impose restraints on those who conform not in all points to their notions of what the Master's work is, and how it is to be promoted, and even to call fire from heaven on those who follow not with them. You must display nothing of the morose and gloomy, nothing of the vain conceits, prejudices, and party ends of sectarianism, nothing of the defects of asceticism on the one hand, or of the superfluity of the frivolous and vain on the other; but ever breathing the Spirit, and acting on the principles of Christ, in imitation of His life, you will let your light so shine before men, that they may behold your good deeds, and glorify your Father which is in heaven. And thus you will receive the truth in the love of it, and exemplify its power in seeking your own and the good of others.

In fine, you must be careful in all your intercourse with men to show them that godliness is profitable unto all things, having the promise of the life that now is, as well as of that which is to come, that the grace which is in Christ Jesus leads you to attend to the personal and relative, the domestic, social, and rational well-being of all men, to the cleanliness of the person, wholesomeness of the diet, suitability of clothing, commodiousness, ventilation, and comfort of the dwelling, to mental cultivation, and social progress; in short, to all things pertaining to the health, prosperity, and comfort of society. In your honest, upright, and generous conduct, you will prove to all around you that Christian principle leads you to shun the vain and frivolous reveries of the diseased brain, and give yourselves to that which prompts you to exercise yourselves in acquiring the knowledge of facts, principles, laws, operations, and results of the physical, rational, and spiritual of being and life.

In the social you will cultivate the spirit of brotherly kindness in a meek and gentle bearing towards all men. In the national you will seek the good of each and every member of the community,—living, as much as lieth in you, peaceably with all men; and while you endeavour in your walk and conversation to exhibit what the grace of God can accomplish in you, and enable you to do for others, you will at the same time make no claim to merit, but will be ever ready to testify that by "the grace of God you are what you are," that not you, "but His grace in you," enables you to live such a life. And that Christianity is not responsible for any shortcomings in your conduct, you must ever be ready to exemplify to others, that while Christianity is perfectly able to make all her disciples shine in the peerless beauty of a perfect holiness, she actually does enable them so to live only in the exact measure in which they individually breathe her spirit, act on her principles, and manifest her power—that it is only in the life of her Lord Himself that she is responsible for the full exhibition of what she can accomplish in man.

Let not truth-seekers be stumbled and turned aside from their search into the nature and evidence of Christianity by the shortcomings of her disciples. They are to bear in mind that the disciples are but in their infant, sickly, or partially trained condition of Christian life here below. They are not to forget that infancy, sickness, and inexperience will display their imperfections; and if such be but properly understood, they will be seen to afford fair opportunities to the more advanced and healthy to display brotherly kindness in the imitation of their Lord, who in His meekness and gentleness seized such opportunities of displaying His generosity and true Christian character. The witnessing of the imperfections of Christians should not turn you away from Christianity itself, and those who allow it to do so only display greater weakness. When we see the sick refuse, or fail to derive the proper benefit from, the food they partake of, we do not refuse to take ours. When we see the infirm unable to discharge the duties of their callings in life, we do not conclude that we should not endeavour to discharge ours; and why should the imperfections of weak or inconsistent Christians turn us away from Christianity?

Let then the Christian ever bear in mind that it is in this world of sin that he possesses his favourable opportunities, that he inherits an ambitious nature, that ambition, allied with selfishness, may perform the most stupendous deeds, reach the highest pinnacle of the Temple of Fame, but must fail in the end of the enjoyment sought in the consciousness of success in benevolent deeds; while ambition, animated by the spirit of self-sacrifice, is not only in itself the most Divine and godlike, but the Divine and godlike that the human can breathe and act on, and being such, will not only in this world secure the highest rewards, but in the world to come the sovereignty of universal empire.

THE END.

Hazell, Watson, and Viney, Printers, London and Aylesbury.

BY THE REV. JOHN COOPER.

VITAL TRUTHS
FOR PRESENT DAY THINKERS.

A Series of Volumes on the most pressing Religious Questions of the Day, in which Evangelical Christianity is recast in unsectarian form. A contribution to the Reunion of the Churches.

I.

THE PROVINCE OF LAW IN THE FALL AND RECOVERY OF MAN; or, *The Law of the Spirit of Life in Contrast with the Law of Sin and Death.* Crown 8vo, Cloth. Price 6s.

II.

THE MODE IN WHICH CHRIST PRESENTED HIMSELF TO THE WORLD. A Proof of His Divine Mission and Supernatural Work. An Original Demonstration of the Truth of Christianity. Crown 8vo, Cloth. Price 6s.

III.

SELF-SACRIFICE THE GRANDEST MANIFESTATION OF THE DIVINE, AND THE TRUE PRINCIPLE OF CHRISTIAN LIFE; or, *The Lost Power of Christian Zeal Restored to the Church.* Crown 8vo, Cloth. Price 6s.

LONDON:
HODDER & STOUGHTON, 27, PATERNOSTER ROW.

NEW AND CHEAPER EDITION OF

DR. PRESSENSÉ'S
EARLY YEARS OF CHRISTIANITY.

In Four Volumes. Price 7s. 6d. each, Handsomely Bound.

The Volumes may be had separately, as follows:—

I.
THE APOSTOLIC AGE. With Portrait.
Crown 8vo, 7s. 6d.

II.
THE MARTYRS AND APOLOGISTS.
Crown 8vo, 7s. 6d.

III.
HERESY AND CHRISTIAN DOCTRINE.
Crown 8vo, 7s. 6d.

IV.
LIFE AND PRACTICE IN THE EARLY CHURCH.
Crown 8vo, 7s. 6d.

"A series in which Dr. Pressensé has undertaken to describe the history of the Church during the first three centuries of the Christian era. His style is good, often eloquent, always perspicuous. It brings out the varying phases of belief which prevailed in the earliest centuries, without indulging in harsh condemnation. The translation is good, and reads well."—*Athenæum.*

"A most valuable and important addition to our Church histories."—*Sunday Magazine.*

"A most fascinating and trustworthy history of the struggles of the early Church, narrated in a style of lofty and impassioned eloquence."—*English Churchman.*

BY THE SAME AUTHOR.

Seventh Edition, unabridged. Crown 8vo, 7s. 6d.

Jesus Christ: His Times, Life, and Work.

In issuing a seventh edition of this important work, the Publishers desire to point out the leading features which distinguish it from other Lives of our Lord. More than one-third of the volume is occupied with a full discussion of "Preliminary Questions," including—1. Objections to the Supernatural; 2. Jesus Christ and the Religions of the Past; 3. The Judaism of His Time; 4. The Sources of the Gospel History. Having thus described His relation to ancient and contemporary history, the author proceeds to unfold the life of Jesus, depicting its scenes with a vividness derived from a visit to the Holy Land. The result is a work which has been referred to by Canon Liddon, as "a most noble contribution to the cause of truth," and by the *Contemporary Review* as "one of the most valuable additions to Christian literature which the present generation has seen."

LONDON:
HODDER & STOUGHTON, 27, PATERNOSTER ROW.

THOMAS COOPER'S
LECTURES ON CHRISTIANITY.

I. **THE BRIDGE OF HISTORY OVER THE GULF OF TIME.** A Popular View of the Historical Evidence for the Truth of Christianity. Seventeenth Thousand. Fcap. 8vo, 2s. 6d.

"The present volume is in his best manner, and deserves to be scattered as men fling seed into the furrows, by handfuls. With God's blessing it will reclaim the sceptical and confirm the wavering."—*Rev. C. H. Spurgeon.*

II. **GOD, THE SOUL, AND A FUTURE STATE.** A Twofold Popular Treatise. Containing (1) the Combined Argument for the Being and Attributes of God; and (2) the Argument for Man's Spiritual Nature and for a Future State. Seventh Thousand. 2s. 6d. cloth.

"There is no living writer that reminds us more forcibly of Paley than the author of these pages,—so plain and simple as he is in his style, so pertinent and close in his reasoning, and so full of apt illustrations are his arguments."—*Standard.*

III. **THE VERITY OF CHRIST'S RESURRECTION FROM THE DEAD.** An Appeal to the Common Sense of the People. Fourth Thousand. Fcap. 8vo, 2s. 6d.

"The thousands of people who have heard the lectures contained in this volume will need no recommendation from us to obtain and peruse them. They will already know how firmly knit is the argument, how eloquent the exposition, how earnest the tone by which they are characterised."—*Christian World.*

IV. **THE VERITY AND VALUE OF THE MIRACLES OF CHRIST.** An Appeal to the Common Sense of the People. Price 2s. 6d. cloth.

"Plain and forcible. Thomas Cooper is a born reasoner. His works on the Evidences are far more likely to be read and to be useful than more elaborate and tedious volumes. By thousands will he be remembered as one of the best popular defenders of the faith."—*Sword and Trowel.*

V. **EVOLUTION, THE STONE, BOOK, AND THE MOSAIC RECORD OF CREATION.** Third Thousand. Price 2s. 6d.

"The great subjects to which they are devoted are handled firmly, liberally, and reverently, and in the best way for the classes to whom they are addressed."—*Church Bells.*

Now ready, the Twelfth Thousand of
THE LIFE OF THOMAS COOPER.
WRITTEN BY HIMSELF.
Crown 8vo, 3s. 6d., with Portrait.
"A most interesting volume."—*Leisure Hour.*

LONDON:
HODDER & STOUGHTON, 27, PATERNOSTER ROW.

WORKS BY REV. SAMUEL COX,

Editor of "The Expositor."

I.

Crown 8vo, cloth, 8s. 6d.

EXPOSITORY ESSAYS AND DISCOURSES.

"A new series of *Expository Essays and Discourses*, by SAMUEL COX, deserves the most cordial welcome we can accord to it. A more helpful book for students and ministers it would not be easy to find. Mr. Cox has a genius for exposition which is very rare. He unites with spiritual insight a keen critical faculty, and a familiarity with the Scriptures which is the result of long and careful research. His books are not only instructive, but stimulating, and are in fact the treasures which the thoughtful preacher will most highly prize, and to which he will give the most honoured place on his shelves."—*The Congregationalist.*

II.

Third Edition, Crown 8vo, cloth, price 8s. 6d.

BIBLICAL EXPOSITIONS.

"The tone of these homilies is wonderfully vigorous, and their standard surprisingly high. There are always the outlines of earnest and laborious thought to be traced under his most impassioned passages; and so far as we have seen, he never quits a subject without illuminating it."—*Literary Churchman.*

"The production of a thoughtful, learned, and liberally-minded man. Mr. Cox's volume is full of valuable matter, well thought out, and lucidly expressed."—*Spectator.*

III.

Fifth Edition, crown 8vo, 8s. 6d.

AN EXPOSITOR'S NOTE-BOOK.

"Mr. Cox's exegetical conscientiousness, fresh and unconventional thinking, tender sentiment, and fine literary taste, give a value to his papers which thoughtful minds and weary hearts will appreciate. We have only commendations for such a book."—*British Quarterly Review.*

LONDON:
HODDER & STOUGHTON, 27, PATERNOSTER ROW.

www.ingramcontent.com/pod-product-compliance
Lightning Source LLC
Chambersburg PA
CBHW022022240426
43667CB00042B/1061